HUMAN RIGHTS
AND
THE WORLD TODAY

HUMAN RIGHTS AND THE WORLD TODAY

Editor

Arundhati Bhattacharyya

KALPAZ

First Published, 2018

Published by

Kalpaz Publications
C-30, Satyawati Nagar,
Delhi – 110052
Ph.: 011-47034999, 9811692060
www.kalpazpublications.com
E-mail: kalpaz@hotmail.com

Printed at: G. Print Process, Delhi

Cataloging in Publication Data—DK
Courtesy: D.K. Agencies (P) Ltd. <docinfo@dkagencies.com>

Human rights and the world today / editor, Arundhati Bhattacharyya.
pages cm
Contributed articles.
Includes bibliographical references.
ISBN 9789353240011

1. Human rights—India. 2. Human rights. I. Bhattacharyya, Arundhati, editor.

LCC JC599.I4H86 2018 | DDC 323.0954 23

Dedicated to
Ma & Baba
for being the
Rock Solid Support
Throughout my Life

Contents

Acknowledgement

I am really thankful to all the contributors of the papers of this editorial venture of mine. They readily consented to contribute chapter for *Human Rights and the World Today*. Their works have helped me to get new insights into the multi-faceted layers of human rights.

I am indebted to all the educational institutions and the renowned teachers I have got the opportunity to learn from. My teachers from my school, St Joseph's Convent, faculties of Presidency College (now Presidency University), Kolkata, faculties of School of International Studies, Jawaharlal Nehru University, New Delhi; where they showed the path to get new insights into the international terrain and Department of Political Science, University of Calcutta for my Ph D.

The institutions where I have worked in, have all contributed to my learning.

My Ph D supervisor, Prof. (Dr) Sonali Chakravarti Banerjee, Vice Chancellor, University of Calcutta has always inspired me to work on my own and instilled confidence in me to go ahead in my academic endeavours.

I have learnt a lot from Dr Minakshi Ray, Pro-Vice Chancellor (BA &V), University of Calcutta.

Prof. (Dr) Anuradha Mukhopadhyay, Vice Chancellor, Diamond Harbour Women's University has also motivated me. I am also thankful to the administration and the support staff of Diamond Harbour Women's University.

Interactions with my students have provided lot of insights into the subjects of International Relations, Human Rights and Political Science.

I am indebted to my family and friends who have stood by me in all situations.

Most importantly, my Ma, Mrs Lily Bhattacharya and my Baba, Mr Amitabha Bhattacharyya have been always been the rock-solid support. Words cannot convey the gratitude I have for them for being my parents.

I am also thankful to the support from the libraries of Diamond Harbour Women's University, West Bengal Commission for Women, Women Studies Research Centre, University of Calcutta, and the British Council.

Finally, I acknowledge my regards to the Publishers who have agreed promptly to publish this work. Their active and effective support have made the process of publication quite smooth.

Preface

This book was planned while teaching a course for the Masters students in Diamond Harbour Women's University. It is a peer-reviewed publication by faculties of Universities. The enquiries raised by the students provoked me to get into the initiation of the book proposal. There is plethora of books on human rights, but a book that would provide the picture from those who are attached as academicians and engaged in scholarly discussion, would add to the resource base and satisfy enquiries regarding the subject matter.

As a student and faculty of International Relations, i believe that protection of human rights is supposed to be the end of every stakeholder. But, the reality is that the precious life of human beings are damaged or harmed every day. There is need to address the issues of violations in order to remind that every life is precious. No one has the right to impinge on the rights of others.

I am grateful to Dr M. K. Srivastava, NIRD, Guwahati; Dr Papiya Dutta, University of Science and Technology, Meghalaya and Ms Channamma Mondal, Bankura University for their support.

I own up every error that may have crept in. i would really appreciate comments and suggestions for further enrichment and updating of the work.

List of Contributors

Goutam Majumder (Ph D) is an Associate Professor, Department of Political Science, Lal Baba College, Belur, Howrah and teaches Political Science in Rabindra Bharati University, Kolkata. He has edited books, and widely contributed papers in books and journals. He has also completed UGC-Minor Research Project.

Molly Ghosh (Ph D) is an Assistant Professor in Political Science at Barrackpore Rastraguru Surendranath College. She has obtained doctoral degree from Jadavpur University and has research interest in gender issues particularly media and women, feminine sexuality and gender violence. She has also made research publications and presentations in several seminars and workshops.

Chandan Roy, (Ph D) an Assistant Professor and Head, Department of Economics, Kaliyaganj College, Uttar Dinajpur, West Bengal, has obtained doctoral degree from University of North Bengal. He contributed to Uttar Dinajpur District Human Development Report-2010 under the aegis of Planning Commission, Government of India and published 25 papers in national and international referred journals and books. He edited several books. His areas of interest are Women Empowerment, Regional Issues of Development and Sericulture Sector.

Susmita Chatterjee (Ph D) is Assistant Professor in Economics, Maharaja Manindra Chandra College Kolkata and Visiting Professor of Department of Commerce,

University of Calcutta for M Phil PhD Course Work. She has graduated from Lady Brabourne College. Her Masters, M. Phil and Ph. D degree are from Calcutta University. Her Post Doctoral research work is from IIMC. Her publications are from Springer, Emerald, Sage etc.

James Okolie-Osemene, a Lecturer in the Department of International Relations, and Co-ordinator, General Studies Unit, Wellspring University Benin City, Nigeria and Research Fellow, IFRA-Nigeria; holds Master of Arts degree in Peace and Conflict Studies from University of Ibadan and Bachelor of Arts degree in History and International Studies from Imo State University, Nigeria. He is undertaking doctoral studies with focus on human rights violations. He is widely published in local and international peer reviewed scholarly journals and contributed chapters to several peer reviewed books. He is Associate Member of the Society for Peace Studies and Practice.

Susmita Bhattacharyya (Ph D) is an Assistant Professor in the Department of Sociology of University of Calcutta. She has her Masters degree in Sociology from University of Calcutta. Her areas of interest are Cultural Studies, Sociology of literature, Sociology of Music, Sociology of Dance and so on.

Sutapa Ghosh (Ph D) is a faculty of the Department of Sociology of Barrackpore Rastraguru Surendranath College, West Bengal. She has doctoral degree from Kalyani University. Her arena of specialisation includes sociology of human rights especially children's rights, sociology of care, motherhood, family, culture, diversity and studies relating to development-security interface. She has contributed articles to different edited volumes besides having edited a book.

Keya Bagchi graduated from Presidency College with an Honours degree in Sociology and her Masters in Sociology from University of Calcutta. She also obtained B.Ed.

degree from Gour Banga University in Malda. She has experience in working with several NGOs on the issues like HIV/AIDS, domestic violence and RCH in Kolkata and Malda. She also worked as tele-counsellor on 1097.

Rita Datta (aka. Rwita Dutta) teaches Political Science in a college under the West Bengal State University. She is editing a book on Indian Regional Films. She is the Editor of an international film journal www.filmbuff.co.in. She is working on her doctoral thesis titled 'City and Cinema'. She has visited many countries to deliver lectures and to take part in seminars and symposiums.

Introduction

— Arundhati Bhattacharyya

Eleanor Roosevelt presented the Universal Declaration of Human Rights to the United Nations by stating "We stand today at the threshold of a great event both in the life of the UN, and in the life of mankind". However, all round the world there are incidents of human rights violations taking place, where even children are not being spared from torture. Doctors or aid workers are not being spared when they are engaged in humanitarian assistance. (Foulkes, 2016) In Mexico, 30, 000 people were missing; in Haiti, there has been deadly hurricane which has created humanitarian crisis, where 60,000 people were living in displacement camps; 36 countries sent refugees back to a country where their rights were at risk; human rights defenders are not getting State protection in Brazil, Venezuela, Honduras, Guatamela, El Salvador, Peru, Ecuador, China, Malaysia, Maldives, Nepal, North Korea, Timor-Leste and elsewhere; Afghanistan remains the second largest origin point of refugees; tens of thousands of Rohingya refugees are fleeing Myanmar; strict measures are being undertaken by the countries of the European Union regarding asylum system; violent terrorist attacks are taking place in France, Germany, United Kingdom etc. This has led to paradigmatic shift in the ways of the States, where measures are being undertaken to restrict human rights in order to provide security. An array of counter-terrorist measures is re-crafting the boundaries between the State and the individual. Yemen, being the poorest country in the Middle

East, is facing armed conflict. Around 2 million children are malnourished and 18.8 million people are in dire need of humanitarian protection. Yazidi women have been facing inhuman violence in the hands of the forces of Islamic States. (Amnesty International Report 2016/17: The State of the World's Human Rights, 2017) Recently, in Venezuela, security forces and pro-government groups have killed around 73 protesters. The United Nations has also criticised the excessive use of power by the authority. (Venezuela: UN rights chief decries excessive force used against protesters, 2017) Crises in Venezuela have brought in scarcity for essential medicines, which is creating havoc for patients. (Tran, 2017)

Man being born free is supposed to enjoy human rights from birth. Human rights are not the gift of modernity to mankind. (Pathak, Promoting Human Rights: The UN Record, 2009) All the religious texts support human rights. The notion of 'natural right' was developed by the Greek philosophers. The overall personality of an individual develops only when an individual has the freedom to enjoy the inherent rights.

In the times of the World War I, human rights were conceived as the exclusive preserve of the State. Things started changing in the inter-war period. The International Labour Organisation started taking steps to protect rights of the workers. Human rights provision was not included in the Versailles Conference and by the drafters of the Covenant of the League of Nations.

Initiatives were also taken during this period by the League of Nations Minorities System, though it lacked universality. The real jolt came from Hitler in the World War II. So, in the post Second World War period, we find that in 1948 the Universal Declaration of Human Rights was a serious move undertaken, for protecting international principles of human rights. The Nuremberg trials (1945-46) disclosed cruelty that had been committed, which was dangerous for human kind. The crimes conducted against peace and humanity should not be repeated anywhere and at anytime in world history. The trials were considered to be water shed for the creation of International Court of Justice and the later Convention on Genocide. (Donnelly, International Human Rights: A Regime Analysis, 1986)

In the formative stage of drafting the Charter of the United Nations, passing reference of human rights was given in the Dumbarton Oaks proposals. In the San Francisco Conference, smaller States and non government organisations persuaded for inclusion of human rights. Finally, there is reference of human rights seven times in the Charter.

The Economic and Social Council has been authorized by Article 62 "to make recommendation for the purpose of promoting respect for and observance of human rights and fundamental freedoms for all" and Article 68 directs the council to "set up a commission for the promotion of human rights". Finally under Article 76, the human rights goal of the United Nations has been pronounced as one of the basic objectives of trusteeship. (Pathak, Promoting Human Rights: The UN Record, 2009)

What are Human Rights?

Human rights provide the individual the basic pre-requisites to develop one's personality and capacities. Human rights are the equal and inalienable rights, in the strong sense of entitlements that ground particularly powerful claims against the State that each person has simply as a human being. They are indivisible rights. Graefrath, Bernhard stated that international human rights standards "can be adapted to any legal system". (Rhoda E. Howard, Jack Donnelly, 1986) The full rainbow of human rights involves respect, protection and fulfilment of civil, cultural, economic, political and social rights, as well as the right to development. (Human Rights, Terrorism and Counter-terrorism: Human Rights Fact Sheet No. 32, 2008)

Wars have been fought in the guise of protection of human rights of groups, communities or nations. Professor Amartya

Sen, the Nobel laureate has stated that human right has gained a new popularity in the language of national and international communication. It has acquired legitimacy in the world parlance. The Universal Declaration of Human Rights has been stated to be the International Bill of Rights. The universality of the rights is hardly appreciated throughout the world. It is culture-specific. However, human rights need legal recognition. Right is a child of law. Legitimacy is equally required. The role of the law enforcement authorities is equally important. But, human rights can go beyond legislation.

The total range of human rights includes International Covenant on Economic, Social and Cultural Rights, and the International Covenant on Civil and Political Rights and its two Optional Protocols. Other core universal human rights treaties are the International Convention on the Elimination of All Forms of Racial Discrimination; the Convention on the Elimination of All Forms of Discrimination against Women and its Optional Protocol; the Convention against Torture and other Cruel, Inhuman or Degrading Treatment or Punishment and its Optional Protocol; the Convention on the Rights of the Child and its two Optional Protocols; the International Convention on the Protection of the Rights of All Migrant Workers and Members of Their Families; the International Convention for the Protection of All Persons from Enforced Disappearance, and the Convention on the Rights of Persons with Disabilities and its Optional Protocol, which were all adopted in December 2006. There is continuous growth of subject-specific treaties and protocols. There are also various regional treaties on the protection of human rights and fundamental freedoms. Customary international law has also binding impact on the State. The right to life is an inherent right, which is the most fundamental right. The Human Rights Committee has observed that this right to life is the supreme one from which no derogation is permitted even during the times of public emergency. Even during the times of war, the right to life inalienable. So, we find that the Geneva

Conventions of 1949 governing the laws of war protect the right to life of civilians and combatants who are injured or have laid down their arms.

The rights recognized in the International Bill of Human Rights are equality of rights without discrimination, life, liberty and security of person, protection against slavery, protection against torture and cruel and inhuman punishment, recognition as a person before the law, equal protection of the law, access to legal remedies for rights violations, protection against arbitrary arrest or detention, hearing before an independent and impartial judiciary, presumption of innocence, protection of privacy, family and home, freedom of movement and residence, freedom of thought, conscience and religion, freedom of opinion, expression and the press, political participation, social security etc. (Donnelly, Human Rights, 2014)

In 1994, the General Assembly's Declaration on Measures to Eliminate International Terrorism, stated that terrorism includes "criminal acts intended or calculated to provoke a state of terror in the general public, a group of persons or particular persons for political purposes" and that such acts "are in any circumstances unjustifiable, whatever the considerations of a political, philosophical, ideological, racial, ethnic, religious or other nature that may be invoked to justify them."

In 2004, the Security Council, in its resolution 1566, referred to "criminal acts, including against civilians, committed with the intent to cause death or serious bodily injury, or taking of hostages, with the purpose to provoke a state of terror in the general public or in a group of persons or particular persons, intimidate a population or compel a Government or an international organization to do or to abstain from doing any act". (Human Rights, Terrorism and Counter-terrorism: Human Rights Fact Sheet No. 32, 2008)

Terrorism And Human Rights

The definition of human rights has gone into re-evaluation

after the lurking fear of terrorism has increased. Terrorism has direct impact on human rights. Due to terror, individuals fail to enjoy the right to life, liberty and property. States also fail to provide security to the individual, which is its basic obligation.

In its drive to containing terrorism, some States are indulging in counter-terrorism. Serious human rights abuses have occurred, which may be the seed for rise of future terrorists. This has led to erosion of good governance and decaying of the environment of implementation of human rights. Combating terrorism by the State is necessary, but, it should not lead to greater terrorist act. The global fight against terrorism needs to be based on the Rule of Law and respect of human rights. (Human Rights, Terrorism and Counter-terrorism: Human Rights Fact Sheet No. 32, 2008)

After the September 11 terror attacks, the prominent United States legal scholar Alan Dershowitz stated in favour of legalized torture as a counter-terror tactics. (Falk, Human Rights, 2004) A coercive approach of spreading human rights and democracy by the Western countries abroad would boomerang, in the longrun. Critics argue that United States plea to spread democracy and rights in Iraq and Afghanistan is a mask for exploitative intention. (Falk, Human Rights, 2004) In the name of protection of human rights of few, rights of others should not be violated, at any cost. The concept and implications of the term human rights change in every era. Torture of slaves in the ancient past was not considered wrong, but, according to today's standards, their treatment by their masters was inhuman. So, in order to protect the country from terrorism, States need to be conscious that they are not violating the basic rights of individuals. An effective balance is the need of the hour.

Refugee

A refugee is a person who has been forced to flee his or her country due to persecution, war, violence, or environmental disasters. The world is being evidence to the grave issue of influx of refugees to countries. The world is facing the difficulty of internal displacement. The complicated issues of refugee and internal displacement are turning to be complex. The mass exodus has been due to the unrest in the host countries. The fear and pain are so huge that people are leaving everything and trying to reach as safer destination. The countries are finding it difficult to handle them. Providing asylum is an international concern. (Bhattacharyya, 2017) On the one hand, humanitarian reasons are pushing some leaders to take on the problem with a human face. On the other hand, some leaders are getting swayed by xenophobia of the masses.

The world community has tried to provide solution to refugee problem. In 1951, the Office of the United Nations High Commissioner for Refugees (UNHCR) was established. The refugees also have rights, which need to be recognized. International instruments like 1951 United Nations Convention relating to the Status of Refugees and its 1967 Protocol relating to the Status of Refugees provide protection to the refugees. Human rights need to have a universal application and need to be extended to the refugees and the internally displaced ones.

Cultural Relativism and Human Rights

Cultural relativism has two totally opposite sides- radical cultural relativism and universal relativism. Radical cultural relativism supports that culture is the sole source of the validity of a moral right or rule. Radical universalism, on the other hand, understands that culture is irrelevant to the validity of moral rights and rules. These rights and rules are universally valid. Both these aspects are 'ideal' types. The reality is something that falls within the continuum. The substance of the right interprets the variation. Importance need to be given not only to expectations of the cosmopolitan moral community, but, also to national and sub-national interpretation, while defining rights. There may be certain rights which are universal in nature, which have been included in the Universal Declaration of Human Rights and covenants of International Human Rights down the years. But, allowances need to be allowed for local interpretations.

But, if human rights are for all human beings, then how is it possible that allowances can be allowed, according to time, place or circumstances? This is a question which is really difficult to answer. (Donnelly, Cultural Relativism and Universal Human Rights, 1984) Here, to Jack Donnelly, cultural relativeness can provide some clues for the answer. Culture is a determining factor in socialisation of an individual and the development of personality. The class and the caste system may create certain restrictions of human rights to control the behaviour of individuals. Individuals enjoy rights in relation to society and State.

Human nature has several possibilities. Its limits are set by the culture of the environment and most importantly, by the individual, oneself. So, we find that siblings growing up in the same family and society turn to be totally different from each other. If societal culture would be the determining factor then they are supposed to be the same. But, the reality is that the power of the individual mind regarding creation of boundaries is the real factor, which affects the conception of rights.

Today, in nearly all parts of the world, universality of rights are proclaimed, at least in theory, but, implementation of the human rights are not that universal. Some practices are 'normal' according to local standards, but not for the international communities. It is these interpretations of these rights which create controversies. Jack Donnelly's interpretation that in many societies we find, parallel societies running where traditional and modern meet or cross each other, at times leading to complexities and differences coming up with no possibility of reaching consensus. It is very difficult to accommodate the demands of the conflicting groups.

Diversity and variability are welcome, but, barbarism is the same according to all standards. A Pol Pot or a Hitler will remain a 'villain' by all standards for all ages. The standard of universality needs to be seen through cultural vision of human nature. Interpretation has to go through the prism of ethical values. 1993 Vienna World Conference on Human Rights stated that it is the duty of States to promote and protect all human rights and fundamental freedoms.

Czech jurist Karel Vasak classified human rights into three generations. The first generation rights are concerned with liberty and participation in political life. They were referred as 'blue rights'. The second generation rights were related to equality. The third generation rights are the collective- developmental ones.

Protection of human rights has always been an indicator of the global well-being. Numerous issues can be affecting the human rights' indicators. Wars and civil conflicts can be the worst places for violations of human rights. However, all around the world, even in peace times, there are issues which need immediate concern. Human Rights Watch with alarmingly frequency identifies human rights violations.

International Organizations

The international regime of human rights is centred on the United Nations. Universal Declaration of Human Rights is the Magna Carta. Classification of rights can be done on the basis of personal (Articles 8-12), civil (Articles 13, 18-20), political (Articles 21) subsistence (Articles 25), economic (Articles 22- 24), social and cultural rights (Articles 26-27). International Covenant on Civil and Political Rights and International Covenant on Economic, Social and Cultural Rights are the global international treaties. They have moulded the guideline for the conception of right. The Human Rights Committee, consisting of eighteen independent experts, monitors the implementation of civil and political rights of the parties. The Commission on Human Rights contribute to monitoring and promotional aspects of human rights. (Donnelly, International Human Rights: A Regime Analysis, 1986)

The United Nations Special Rapporteur on extreme poverty and human rights, Philip Alston, has called on the World Bank and its member States to adopt a new and consistent approach to human rights. "For most purposes, the World Bank is currently a human rights-free zone. In its operational policies, in particular, it treats human rights more like an infectious disease than universal values and obligations," Alston states this in a new report published online on the approach to human rights by the World Bank, the most important international actor on poverty alleviation. ("The World Bank is a Human Rights-Free Zone" – UN expert on extreme poverty expresses deep concern', 29 September 2015,, 2015)

In order to make the world safe, a Treaty on the Prohibition of Nuclear Weapons at the United Nations was adopted in 2017. The aim is to address the humanitarian consequences of using and testing nuclear weapons. The fight started after destruction took place in Hiroshima and Nagasaki. (Docherty, 2017)

Kenneth Roth, the Executive Director of Human Rights Watch state that in the name of majority, decisions are being undertaken which has gone against the rights of the refugees, immigrant population or the minorities. Xenophobia has increasingly spread in this decade. Respect for protection of human rights in several parts of the globe is seeing a downturn. This can lead to a shady foundation of safe, independent and prosperous communities.

Migration due to push factors has become a grave matter of concern for the international community. The entry of migrants is intertwined with the complex impact it has on the identity, racism, possibility of long term socio-economic-cultural repercussions on the host society. The threat of terrorism on the North and the South is creating greater concern for security, which at times, is impacting the rights, even in the private sphere. The fear of the unknown is creating greater doubts on the 'outsiders', who are taking refuge in the refugee camps.

It is rather difficult to identify with people who are 'different'. Violation of their rights is easily accepted.

Globalization, Multiculturalism and Human Rights

The gap is increasing between the feelings of 'us' and 'them' among the native population, which is questioning the real sense of globalisation in the current era. Selective implementation of human rights is being undertaken, where the rights of 'others' can be compromised easily. Human rights violated at any level will shake its foundation. Human rights are not unlimited. It is inextricable related to duties.

The global economic downturn had impacted the lives of migrants negatively. Vulnerability of the migrants and their families has been affected adversely. Just as free movement of goods is desirable in a globalized world, similarly free of people should also be appreciated. Low-skilled workers are not much aware of accessing information regarding emigration. The lack of information creates a field day for scrupulous people. The government can assist them through information help desk and skilling them so that they get better opportunities abroad. They may save themselves from smuggling and trafficking. (Gurucharan, 2013)

The global refugee crisis could not be solved by world leaders. States even did not attend the United Nations' summit for refugees and migrants. 75,000 refugees remained trapped in a desert no man's land between Syria and Jordan. In African countries like Cameroon, Central African Republic (CAR), Chad, Niger, Nigeria, Somalia, South Sudan and Sudan, there have been widespread human rights violations. This again led to internal displacement and aggravated the refugee crises. Gender-based violence has occurred where women and girls had to face violence. It is a matter of concern that the African Union had proclaimed 2016 as the year of human rights, but member States failed to actualize it. (Amnesty International Report 2016/17: The State of the World's Human Rights, 2017)

The continuous attack on migrants for 'stealing' jobs may be unfounded as they perform many menial jobs which the citizens of the country keep away from. The smooth functioning of the economy is possible due to their contribution. The easier it is accepted, the better will be the level of tolerance towards them.

Multinational companies may violate human rights. When people protested, crack downs were ordered against them. Transparency and accountability are lacking. Muscle power-control has also threatened protection of human rights.

'Climate refugee' is a matter of concern. Thomas Homer-Dixon and Norman Dyers have been emphasising on environmental refugees turning into serious issue. The Paris agreement recognised the significance of migration. In several parts, there is rise in the sea level, which is creating havoc for the coastal areas.

The environment to have faith in human rights is dipping in every part of the world, including the West. But, leaders like Angela Merkel, Justin Trudeau and former United States President, Barack Obama have kept their standards high even today, regarding recognition of human rights. Governments committed to protection of human rights have a transparent and accountable society- State interface, which in the long run is beneficial for the larger interest of the people.

Multiculturalism enhances the vibrancy of any society. But, not accepting to 'agree to disagree' aggravates the intolerance and discrimination among the 'haves' and the 'have nots'. State needs to treat every person with dignity. The framework of human rights can be the foundation of the relationship between the individual and the State. The yardstick of the liberal State depends on the human rights enjoyed by the inhabitants, including citizens and aliens.

In different countries, intolerance is seeping in the cleavages of the societies, overtly and covertly. This is aggravating the level of conflicts at every layer. Peace is missing. Tendency of intolerance and authoritarianism has increased round the globe. In some countries, politicians have justified hostility towards immigrants. Autocrats have forced farmers, in places, to vacate for megaprojects. In many countries, the military junta have overthrown the democratically elected governments.

Civil wars have aggravated violation of human rights. War crimes have made the life of the civilians difficult, though ethically, attacking civilians is prohibited. But, even hospitals are being destroyed and attacked. Civilians have been displaced in many corners of the world. They have run away to neighbouring countries in search of security. For the sake of selfish interest, some individuals and sections of society are making the world a very scary space to live in.

The civil society organisations can increase liberal space. Bridging North-South divide is necessary.

The civil society has the responsibility of protecting civic space. Lessons from North and South need to be learned in order to oppose autocrats. The neutral media has great strength to reverberate the importance of implementation of human rights through propaganda. 'Fake news' needs to be counteracted; actively and continuously. This would prevent destruction of lives of others.

Eternal vigilance is the price of liberty. Ultimately, it is the public who has the responsibility to protect their rights. Protection of human rights furthers the feeling of showing empathy to the rights and needs of others. (Roth, 2017)

Poverty and Human Rights

Hunger and poverty is the greatest obstacle for enjoyment

of human rights. The alternate view of poverty which inspires bottom-up, value-laden, indigenous and participatory approach, has defined poverty as a situation suffered by people who are not able to meet their material and non-material needs through their own effort.

In the post 1945 period, a global food regime has come into being. Transnational corporations are playing an important link in this food regime. Subsistence farming for the local consumption is being discouraged. Genetically modified products are being marketed widely in the developing world. Cash crop production is being affected by the economy. Green revolution may have yielded high production, but has thrown away millions of farmers out of labour. Environmental impacts of use of fertilisers, pesticides etc have ecological damages. During the 1980s and 1990s, inequalities in the global level have been furthered by the worldwide promotion of the neo-liberal economic policies. Structural adjustment programmes have been introduced in the national economies. Even after massive production of food grains, people are dying of hunger and malnutrition. So, there are matters regarding improper distribution of food. Access and entitlement are influenced by factors, like North-South divide, dichotomy of urban-rural access, caste, class, gender, race etc. On the one hand, there is excessive food production and the other, many people are killed due to hunger and poverty. (Thomas, 2001)

Malnutrition and malnourishment have prevented many souls to enjoy the basic human rights. Poverty can nullify all economic, social, political rights. Poor fail to enjoy the rights, like right to pursue education, right to health, right to practise any profession etc. They, in turn, become the marginalised and disadvantaged in the society. World poverty cannot be solved through rhetoric. Discrimination in dealing with the poor becomes an obstacle to alleviate poverty. It has deep laden impact on enjoyment of human rights. Both direct and indirect discrimination have its own repercussions.

Inequality reduction helps in ending extreme poverty. The twin aims of the World Bank are to reduce extreme poverty to 3 per cent or less of the global population by 2030 and boosting shared prosperity, i.e., promoting consumption or income growth of the bottom 40 per cent in every country. These two goals are complementary to each other. 80 per cent of the global poor live in the rural areas. Two-thirds of them depend on agriculture. 50 per cent of the global poor are children. There are regional differences in the concentration of the poor. In order to arrest poverty, six policy areas need to be focussed. They are early childhood development and nutrition; universal health care; quality education; conditional cash transfers; rural infrastructure investments and taxation. (Revenga, 2016)

The World Bank is committed to include gender equality as a way to deal with alleviation of poverty in the world.

Gender Equality is a Human Right

Discrimination on the basis of gender is a practice in many societies of the world. It is considered to be nothing wrong. Giving less food and care to the girl child is a norm in many cultures. Girls face double or intersecting challenges to their rights.

The Gender Inequality Index (GII) ranks countries on the levels of gender inequality in reproductive health, empowerment and economic status. Greater the level of inequality, greater is the GII.

Now, it is the time that the orthodox norms and conventions need to be rooted out.

Feminization of poverty is a reality. The relationship between gender and poverty is a complex phenomenon. Targeting women has become one vehicle for gender-sensitive poverty alleviation. (Cagatay, 1998)

According to UNICEF, 230 million children under the age of 5 lack a birth certificate, overwhelmingly in Asia and sub-

Saharan Africa. Without a birth certificate, a child will surely face difficulties in life. It can range from enrolment in school, to accessing health and other social services, and even in securing a job and inheriting property. Just a lack of piece of paper may lead to so many hiccups for the child later.

Quality education is a human right for all. But, the probability is that access to it is less for girls than for boys. It is a powerful tool for human resource development.

The role of women for development is widely accepted as a path towards poverty alleviation. Gender has gone through its own mainstreaming process. (Bieri, 2009)

When the 2030 Agenda is kept in mind, it is the girl child of 10 years whose development needs to be monitored. They are the population who are most likely to be left behind.

The Convention on the Elimination of All Forms of Discrimination against Women and the Convention on the Rights of the Child are international legal standards that outline rights of girls and women. There is no single legal instrument focused on girls themselves, who, as females and as young people, face dual and intersecting challenges to their rights. (The State of World Population 2016, 2016)

The International Court of Justice (ICJ)

On April 18, 1946, a resolution of the League of Nations terminated the Permanent Court of International Justice. Article 14 of the Covenant of the League of Nations gave the Council of the League responsibility for formulating plans for the establishment of a Permanent Court of International Justice.

After the formation of the United Nations in the post-Second World War, the International Court of Justice started to work as its principal judicial arm. It works independently. It is referred to as the world court. The ICJ is the highest court in the world. It is seated in The Hague. It has both general and universal jurisdiction. It is open to all Member

States of the United Nations. It is subject to the provisions of its Statute and it can entertain any question of international law. (The International Court of Justice: Handbook, 2016) It is composed of fifteen judges. They are elected by the General Assembly and the Security Council of the United Nations. It heavily borrowed from the legacy of the Permanent Court of International Justice. There is a lot of controversy whether ICJ has been able to implement human rights or humanitarian laws. In ICJ, only the States can bring contentious issues in this platform. Though the Court has been working since the mid-twentieth century, proper application of international human rights law was strengthened in the twenty first century. In 2004, the ICJ ruled in an advisory opinion regarding the legal consequences of a wall constructed by Israel in Palestinian territory under Israeli occupation. It stated that Israel violated the provisions of the Fourth Geneva Convention, 1949, the International Covenant on Civil and Political Rights, the International Covenant on Economic, Social and Cultural Rights and the UN Convention on the Rights of the Child. Similarly, in 2009, the ICJ brought into limelight the jurisprudence of the UN Human Rights Committee. (Sunga, 2016) Simple cases can move quickly, but complex and contested cases can drag on for years, as happened in 1993 in the case between Yugoslavia and Bosnia-Herzegovina. It has also been criticized that some judges give priority to their national identity and national interest, rather than world interest. Few of them have background in direct link towards human rights protection. (Crook, 2004) The International Court of Justice can play a more active role in protection of human rights.

International Criminal Court

International Criminal Court (ICC) was established by the Rome Statute. On 17 July, 1998, 120 States adopted a Statute in Rome. It is for the first time that the countries have decided to accept the jurisdiction of a permanent international criminal court. Mid-2004, sixty six countries ratified the treaty on April 11, 2002. On October 4, 2004, the International Criminal Court and the United Nations signed an agreement governing their institutional relationship. The seat of the court is in The Hague, the Netherlands. There are 18 judges. (Understanding the International Criminal Court, 2012) The International Criminal Court is a permanent international tribunal which is supposed to prosecute crimes against humanity, genocide and war crimes. It is a court of last resort in these fields.

Human rights are valued only if implemented. The Office of the High Commissioner for Human Rights has been assisting and supporting States. It is done through the Technical Cooperation Programme. It is funded through the United Nations Voluntary Fund for Technical Cooperation in the Field of Human Rights. UNHCR assists legislatures to further human rights. It also helps in assistance for the incorporation of international human rights norms in national Constitutions and laws. The Paris Principles was adopted by the General Assembly in 1993. It is the guiding spirit for countries regarding measurement of human rights. (Promotion: the Role of Technical Cooperation, 2003)

Conclusion

The 2030 Agenda for Sustainable Development has been adopted by 193 countries at the United Nations in 2015. It represents a singular moment in the history of global consensus on development. It applies to all countries. It puts forward a course of transformation, grounded firmly in human rights and the inclusion of all individuals. Sustainability is a keyword. Resources that have been utilized wisely now will be available for future generations. The 2030 Agenda focus on achievement of 17 Sustainable Development Goals and 169 targets. No one can be allowed to be left behind, at any cost. It is not optional to respect human rights. It is a mandatory aspect, for every State and non-State actors. Optimism and hope can help to advance with the goals at hand and reach their positively.

Summary of Main Issues of the Contributions

Gautam Majumdar provides analysis of the origin and evolution of human rights from both the oriental and western perspectives. The notion of 'Rights of Man' and other such concepts of rights are as old as humanity. He starts off with Western scholar, Sophocles (495-406 BC), Roman and Greek thinkers, then moves over to Hindu jurists like *Narada, Brhaspati* and *Katayan,* thinkers from Medieval Europe and the role of the United Nations in promoting human rights.

Molly Ghosh discusses Human Rights as a contested concept that kept on evolving with newer insights and focuses on the universality vs. difference debate in the concept of Human Rights and how far this debate has changed the understanding of Human Rights. The idea of human rights is of ancient origin, which is associated with philosophies around the world. The Universal Declaration of Human Rights has stressed on universality of the concept. But, in the late twentieth century, strengthening of views of identity has challenged the notion of universality.

Chandan Roy and Susmita Chatterjee in their paper unravel different right-based dimensions of gendered entrepreneurship in India. The paper justifies the need of female enterprise in the Indian socio-political and cultural space. It contextualises the issue in the economic perspective and locates the gender based dimension of entrepreneurship in the Indian economy explaining the lacunae behind its slow growth; illustrates the constitutional provisions of women entrepreneurs as guaranteed by Indian Constitution; elaborates the actual scenario of women entrepreneurs in Indian economy; assesses the reasons for its strengths and weaknesses; attempts to reason out the gap between actual and ideal position of women entrepreneurs especially from the rights based perspective and suggests some corrective measures as means to go ahead.

James OKOLIE-OSEMENE provides a study on patterns and evolution of human rights abuses during Nigerian Biafran war. The article explores why and how both sides were involved in the violation of citizens' rights to life, freedom of movement and other socio-economic rights. The police action declared by General Gowon marked the beginning of hostilities against secessionist Biafra. Using qualitative data, this is explanatory case study research design. This article maintains that protection mindset had little or no value mainly due to the self determination goal of the Biafran side.

Sutapa Ghosh has got into the details of the growth of children's rights movement in India. They are an asset to the community. Development activities of India should start with the children irrespective of caste, sex, religion and race. The paper deals with international and the national instruments, programmes, schemes and the condition of children in the pre and post-independence period. In the future, the child rights' movement will definitely occupy a strong place in the Indian society. Children are the future of the Indian society, so their human resource development is of primary importance.

Susmita Bhattacharyya deals with human trafficking as a serious social crime, causative factors, impact and the means of prevention, protection, prosecution, rescue, restoration, repatriation, rehabilitation and reintegration of those who fall into the trafficking trap. The 'culture of silence' of the victims of trafficking needs to be transformed into 'zero tolerance' by the State, society and the community. The impacts of trafficking on the victim, the role of the nongovernmental organizations, the strong role of law, etc are discussed in the paper. Holistic effort is required regarding tackling the evil of human trafficking of women.

Keya Bagchi has provided a picture of the violations of human rights in different parts of the world and in India, but, it has focussed mainly on the violations that have happened in West Bengal. It has covered issues, like, crimes against women, including domestic violence; details regarding the push and pull factors, modes and routes in trafficking;

rape; child labour; sexual harassment at workplace; and ended with the relation between human rights and globalisation and some of the ways, by which violation of human rights can be prevented.

Rwita Dutta has delved into the Cinema of Resistance which is a unique concept in the history of films. Though, in theory, human rights are ensured by the Indian Constitution, post-independence era witnessed a total discrimination in the socio-economic system of the country. Thus the trajectory of cinema of resistance has been shifted from "Jai Bhim Comrade", a documentary by Anand Patwardhan to the mainstream full length feature "Parched" by Leena Yadav which created uproar in the popular psyche. The paper analyzes the diversification of film making in India and the interesting mode of resistance through cinematic forms.

References

(2017). *Amnesty International Report 2016/17: The State of the World's Human Rights.* London: Amnesty International.

Bhattacharyya, A. (2017). Refugees and Refugee Reintegration. In P. Joseph, *The SAGE Encyclopedia of War: Social Science Perspectives* (pp. 1446-1449). Thousand Oaks: Sage Publications.

Bieri, S. (2009, March-April 31 March - 2 April 2009). *Power and poverty. Reducing gender inequality by ways of rural employment?* Retrieved August 12, 2017, from OECD: http://www.oecd.org/dac/gender-development/42806451.pdf

Cagatay, N. (1998, May). *Gender and Poverty: Working Paper 5.* Retrieved August 12, 2017, from Gender and Poverty: http://www.pnud.org/content/dam/aplaws/publication/en/publications/poverty-reduction/poverty-website/gender-and-poverty/Gender and Poverty.pdf

Crook, J. R. (2004). The International Court of Justice and Human Rights. *Northwestern Journal of International Human Rights* .

Docherty, B. (2017, July 7). *Treaty Banning Nuclear Weapons Adopted.* Retrieved July 8, 2017, from Human Rights Watch: https://www.hrw.org/news/2017/07/07/treaty-banning-nuclear-weapons-adopted

Donnelly, J. (1984). Cultural Relativism and Universal Human Rights. *Human Rights Quarterly*, 400-419.

Donnelly, J. (2014). Human Rights. In J. Baylis, S. Smith, & P. Owens, *The Globalization of World Politics* (pp. 361-375). Oxford: Oxford University Press.

Donnelly, J. (1986). International Human Rights: A Regime Analysis. *International Organization*, 599-642.

Falk, R. (2004). Human Rights. *Foreign Policy*, 18-28.

Falk, R. (2004). Human Rights. *Foreign Policy*, 18-28.

Foulkes, I. (2016, December 30). *Are we heading towards a 'post human rights world'?* Retrieved July 10, 2017, from BBC: http://www.bbc.com/news/world-europe-38368848

Gurucharan, G. (2013). *The Future of Migration from India Policy, Strategy and Modes of Engagement.* New Delhi: India Centre for Migration, Ministry of External Affairs, Government of India.

(2008). *Human Rights, Terrorism and Counter-terrorism: Human Rights Fact Sheet No. 32.* Geneva: Office of the United Nations High Commissioner for Human Rights, United Nations.

Pathak, V. (2009). Promoting Human Rights : The UN Record . *The Indian Journal of Political Science*, 151-164.

Pathak, V. (2009). Promoting Human Rights: The UN Record. *The Indian Journal of Political Science*, 151-164.

Promotion: the Role of Technical Cooperation. (2003, July 16). Retrieved August 17, 2017, from Office of the High Commissioner for Human Rights: http://www.ohchr.org/Documents/Countries/terrain.pdf

Revenga, A. (2016). *"Taking on Inequality" Poverty and Shared Prosperity 2016.* Retrieved August 11, 2017, from World Bank: http://pubdocs.worldbank.org/en/369011497229488510/061217-PSPR-presentation.pdf

Rhoda E. Howard, Jack Donnelly. (1986). Human Dignity, Human Rights and Political Regimes. *The American Political Science Review*, 801-817.

Sunga, L. S. (2016, April 18). *The International Court of Justice's Growing Contribution to Human Rights and Humanitarian Law.* Retrieved August 14, 2017, from The Hague Institute for Global Justice: http://www.thehagueinstituteforglobaljustice.org/latest-insights/latest-insights/commentary/the-international-court-of-justices-growing-contribution-to-human-rights-and-humanitarian-law/

The International Court of Justice: Handbook. (2016). The Hague: United Nations.

(2016). *The State of World Population 2016.* New York: United Nations Population Fund.

Thomas, C. (2001). Poverty, Development and Hunger. In S. S. John Baylis, *The Globalization of World Politics: An Introduction to International Relations* (pp. 559-581). Oxford: Oxford University Press.

Tran, C. (2017, August 10). *Medicine Shortages in Venezuela: Dying in Agony*. Retrieved August 16, 2017, from Human Rights Watch: https://www.hrw.org/news/2017/08/10/medicine-shortages-venezuela-dying-agony

Understanding the International Criminal Court. (2012). The Hague: ICC.

Venezuela: UN rights chief decries excessive force used against protesters. (2017, August 8). Retrieved August 15, 2017, from The Guardian: https://www.theguardian.com/world/2017/aug/08/venezuela-un-rights-chief-decries-excessive-force-used-against-protesters

Chapter - I

Origin and Evolution of Human Rights

— Gautam Majumdar

Introduction

> *Recognition of the inherent dignity and of the equal and inalienable rights of all members of the human family is the foundation of freedom, justice and peace in the world.*
>
> **Preamble, Universal Declaration of Human Rights**

Human Rights are commonly understood as 'inalienable fundamental right' to which a person is inherently entitled simply because he or she is a human being. Irrespective of caste, creed, sex, region, colour, profession and others, humankind must have some rights from birth and these birth rights are nowadays regarded as human rights. They are also somewhere called Fundamental Rights and they may include civil rights, political, economic, cultural and social rights. Human rights are conceived as universal and egalitarian since it denotes right to life, liberty, equality and dignity of an individual against all sorts of injustice, exploitation and disdain.

The term human right is comparatively of recent origin. This 20th Century term is traditionally known as 'Natural

Rights' or in a more appealing phase, the 'Rights of Man'. The notion of 'Rights of Man' and other such concepts of rights are as old as humanity. These rights of men had a place almost in all the ancient societies of the world, though they are not referred to by that time. Hence, the idea of human rights may be claimed to be as old as the history of human civilization. It is deeply rooted in the historical past contrary to the standard histories of the 1948 Universal Declaration of Human Rights that assume consensus and the triumph of human rights during the post-World War II period.

Early Roots of Human Rights

The roots of human rights can be traced to the Babylonian laws. (Wines, 2006) The Babylonian king Hammurabi issued a set of laws to his people called 'Hammurabi's Codes', which contained for fair wages, protection of property and the charges against them to be provided at trial. The Assyrian Laws, the Hittite laws and the Dharma of the Vedic period in India also devised different sets of standards by which the rights of one were respected by another. (Parekh, 2010) A declaration for religious tolerance on an egalitarian basis can be found in the "Edicts of Ashoka", which emphasise the importance of tolerance in public policy by the government. The slaughter and capture of prisoners of war was also condemned by the great Indian emperor. Prophet Muhammad condemned female infanticide, exploitation of poor, usury, murder, false contracts and theft. He also incorporated Arabic and Mosaic laws and customs of the time into his divine revelations. The Constitution of Medina (Charter of Medina) established the security of the community, freedom of religion and security of women. Thus all major religions of the world have a humanist perspective that supports human rights despite the differences in their context.

Western scholars date the genesis of the idea of natural law to Sophocles (495-406 BC), more than 400 years before Christ. He was one of the first to promote the idea of freedom of expression of opinion against the State. A few Greek and

Roman philosophers recognized the idea of natural rights. Plato (427-348 BC) was one of the earliest thinkers to advocate a universal standard of ethical conduct. *The Republic* (400 BC) proposed the idea of universal truths that should be recognized by all. (Nina Redman, Lucille Whalen, 1998) He has also made an important contribution to the development of the conception of necessity of a universal and eternal set of rules regarding human beings. He made a clear distinction between ideas and culture or tradition. His works have a pronounced character of assertion, discovery of human rights and liberties.

Aristotle (384-322 BC) wrote in *Politics* that justice, virtue and rights change in accordance with different kinds of institutions and circumstances. (Miller, 1995) He was the first one in asserting the idea of natural law, by saying that a person becomes slave or free only by law, human beings do not differ at all by the nature of mankind.

Cicero (106-43 BC), a Roman statesman, laid down the foundation of 'natural law' and 'human rights' in his work *The Laws* (52 BC). Cicero believed that there should be universal human rights that transcend customary and civil laws. (Cicero, Rudd, Powell, 1998) According to Roman jurist, Ulpain, natural law was that "which nature and State assure to all human beings". (Desai, 1991) This meant that foreigners must be treated in the same way as one deals with one's compatriots. It also implied conducting of wars in a civilized manner.

The City States of Greece gave freedom of speech, equality before law, right to vote, right to be elected to public office, right to trade and right to access to justice to their citizens. Similar rights were secured by the Romans by "*Jus Civile*" of the Roman Law. Thus, the origin of the concept of human rights can be found in the Greco-Roman natural law doctrines. The Stoics also employed the ethical concept of natural law to refer a higher order of law which correspond to nature and which was to serve as a standard for the laws of civil society and Government. Stoicism, the school of philosophy founded by Zeno and Citium, held that a universal force pervades all creation and that human conduct should, therefore, be judged according to the laws of nature.

The Position of Hindu Jurisprudence

Long before civilization dawned in Egypt and Greece, the Hindu jurists have elaborated the procedures for civil and criminal cases as well as investigations. Hindu jurists like *Narada,Brhaspati* and *Katayan* have elaborated rules to the innocent and stressed the king should not shrink from punishing the guilty. It was laid down that if thieves and robbers have a free run in any kingdom, the king was doomed to eternal damnation in hell. The foremost duty of the state is to protect the citizens from criminals, enemies of the State and from the avarice or greed of the high officials. (Giriraj Shah, K.N. Gupta, 2001)

Thus we find the concept of human rights is not entirely western, Rig Veda cites three civil rights that of *Tana* (Body), *Skridhi* (Dwelling Place) and *Jibhasi* (Life). Mahabharata tells about the importance of the freedoms of the individual (civil liberties) in a state. Concept of D*harma* – rights and duties of individuals, classes, communities and castes – has been delineated in our scriptures. Before second century BC, Indian States could boast of elected kings. Arthasastra elaborates on civil and legal rights first formulated by *Manu* which also included economic rights. (Kumar, 2003)

Human Rights in Medieval Europe

Analysing the historical development of human society, the Christian philosophers of Middle Ages tried to develop ideas about the condition of human equality from the Decalogue with the ten commands, announcing in this way the fundamental individual rights characteristic for any human being. According to the theory of St. Thomas Acquinas (1225-1274), the individual is the centre of a right social and legal order but the divine law has supremacy over the worldly law, such as it is defined by the king. "The Christian Church even established a hierarchy of various law sources in matter, giving priority to the divine law, on second places appearing natural law and only on third place the positive law derived from the primary (divine) and the secondary (natural), being nothing else than common rules of the relationships in society." (Closca, Suceava, 1995)

During the seventeenth century, the exponents of natural law, especially Hugo Grotius, surnamed the father of natural law science, showed that "man is a sociable being by its nature, who wishes to live peacefully with its fellows, able to determine by him on what is useful or harmful for society. (Barsan, 2005) In England, the case for a natural law, superior to man-made law, was argued by Blackstone in this century. He has identified three rights which he aptly remarked to have been 'founded on nature and reason': the right to personal security, the right to personal liberty and the right to property. (Blackstone, 1765) Eighteenth century thinker Montesquieu formulated a definition of law: "Laws, in the most ample sense, are necessary reports derived from the nature of things and in this sense, all the works have their own laws". (Montesquieu, 2005) The quality of Montesquieu is that of having understood in context the relationship between laws and liberty and also the contribution to the ideological preparation of the French Revolution from 1789. This philosophy has a progressive character because, alluding to the essential components of the society, it asserted that "people gave up their natural independence in order to submit civil laws" mentioning, in conclusion that the first laws represent liberty and the last ones property. Rousseau believed that the equality of people consists in the fact that they are similar in dignity, because, the law belonging to all of them is not owned by someone else in particular. Therefore, law must be placed above people and not one man above the other, since equality involves freedom, taking into account that the compliance to a law determined by someone means freedom. (Rousseau, 1762)

The problem of fundamental human rights and liberties remain a constant preoccupation of the great philosophers in the following decades. By the end of the eighteenth century, the problem of human rights passed to a new phase of development – devotion of rights in international documents and became the contemporary system of international law of human fundamental rights and liberties.

Instruments for Human Rights Protection

In medieval Europe, the Magna Carta (1215), the first text known in history, was related to General Charter of Rights. It is not a complete catalogue of civil rights and liberties as we know of today, it could be described as the starting point of Constitutional history which shifted focus from the power of the State to human rights, since it has enshrined the principles of liberty, justice and even of equality and fraternity. (Ahamadi, 2000) It is a great tribute to the people of England to have preserved it, to nurse it over the years to serve as a beacon to humankind. Though the bundle of civil rights and liberties under 'the Magna Carta' was limited, its impact was revolutionary in the sense that it ushered in the realization and recognition that individuals had certain rights and could claim these rights against the state and that the state was expected to respect and not to interfere with such rights and liberties of the individuals.

'The Magna Carta' granted by King John of England to the English barons on June 15, 1215 was in response to the stiff opposition to the heavy burden of taxation created by the third Crusade and the ransom of Richard I, captured by the Holy Emperor Henry VI. The English barons protested against the heavy taxes and were unwilling to let King John rule again without granting some concessions regarding their rights. The overreaching theme of 'Magna Carta' was the protection against arbitrary acts by the King. Accordingly land

and property could no longer be seized, judges had to know and respect laws and taxes could not be imposed without common counsel. There could be no punishment without a trial. The merchants were granted the right to travel freely within and outside England. 'The Magna Carta' also introduced the concept of Jury trial which provided protection against arbitrary arrest and imprisonment. This document was telling that: "No free man could be arrested, imprisoned or dispossessed of his goods, declared against the law, exiled or injured in any matter and we will not be against him or send anyone against him without a loyal judgement of his equals or in conformity with the law of the country. (Barsan, 2005) Thus the Charta set forth the principle that the power of the king was not absolute. During the reign of Henry III, 'The Magna Carta' was confirmed by the British Parliament. Similar to the English 'Magna Carta' the statute of Kalisz (1264) gave privilege to the Jewish minority in the Kingdom of Poland. In 1525, in Germany the peasants put their 'Twelve Articles' i.e. demands towards the 'Swabian League' in the German peasant's war.

The modern sense of human rights can be traced to Renaissance Europe and Protestant Reformation, as also the disappearance of the feudal authoritarianism and the religious conservatism that dominated the Middle Ages. The European wars of religion and civil wars of the 17th century England gave rise to the philosophy of liberalism and belief in human rights became a central concern of European intellectual culture during 18th century 'Age of Enlightenment'. That's why first legal instrument of transposition in legal provisions of the fundamental rights and liberties appeared in the European culture during the 17th -19th century. In England there came out some important documents regarding human rights entitled: The Petition of Rights (1628) which reinforced the Magna Carta; Habeas Corpus Act (1679) and Bill of Rights (1689). Bill of Rights declared the rights and liberties of the subject, like the right to free elections, the freedom of word, the right of release on bail, the prohibition of cruel punishments, the right to be judged by an independent court formed the platform for Parliamentary superiority over the Crown and gave a documentary authority for the 'Rule of Law' in England. And Dicey has demonstrated that rights were derived from rule of law by discussing the right to personal freedom, freedom of discussion and the right to assembly. (Dicey, 1885) The concept of 'fundamental rights of man' is found in the declarations and constitutional instruments of many states. In the United States, the state of Virginia adopted 'the Declaration of Rights from the state of Virginia' (1776) which provided that "all people are born equal, free and independent; they have inherent rights they cannot be deprived of or dispossessed of by any contract, when having social relations, meaning the right to enjoy life and freedom, with the possibility of purchasing and possessing goods and the right to search and obtain happiness and personal security." 'The Declaration of Independence of the United States of America' (1776) was adopted two days after Virginia Declaration in Philadelphia which settled the basic idea that all governances have been established by people in order to guarantee the appointed rights. The Constitution of the United States (1787) with amendments in 1789, 1865, 1869 and 1919 specified a number of rights. Bill of Rights was formally added in 1791. Incorporation of individual rights in a written constitution consequently led to incorporation of human rights into the municipal law of a State, and to make them legally enforceable by an aggrieved individual against his state to invalidate any state act, legislature or executive, which is found by a court of law to have violated any of the constitutionally guaranteed human rights belonging to the aggrieved individual.

The Declaration of the Rights of Man and of the Citizen (1793) is a fundamental document of French Revolution defining the individual and collective rights of all the estates of the realm as universal. It was adopted during the French Revolution in 1789, but after modifications it was adopted in

1793. This Declaration is again in the spirit of natural law which does not base itself on religious doctrine or authority. According to this, "Men are born free and remain free and equal in rights". And hence, the role of government is to recognize and secure these rights. They are liberty, property, security and resistance to oppression. This Declaration led other European states to include provisions in their laws for protection of human rights. Sweden in 1809, Spain in 1812, Norway in 1814, Belgium in 1831, Denmark in 1849, Prussia in 1850 and Switzerland in 1874 made provisions for the fundamental rights of man. The idea of human rights that lay the core of the American and French Revolutions also paved the way for universal adult franchise.

Human Rights in Modern Era

The developments in France were followed by developments in philosophy of human rights by philosophers such as Thomas Paine, John Stuart Mill and Hegel during eighteenth and nineteenth centuries. The term 'human rights' was coined by Thomas Paine and was used first time in the English translation of the French Declaration. Henry David Thoreau in his classic treatise *Civil Disobedience* expanded the concept.

In the nineteenth century human rights became a central concern over the issue of slavery. In Britain, William Wilberforce worked towards it and the result was that Britain passed Slave Trade Act, 1807 and Slavery Abolition Act, 1833. In the United States, northern states already abolished slavery and the southern states did it later.

The establishment of the 'International Committee' of the Red Cross the 'Lieber Code' and the 'Geneva Conventions' in 1864 laid the foundations of International Humanitarian Law.' This is because the term 'Natural Rights' eventually fell into disfavour and the concept of 'Universal Rights' took root. The phrase 'the right of man' was found unsuitable, as it was not universally understood to include the rights of women. Later Eleanor Roosevelt suggested in 1947 that the term 'Rights of Man' be changed to 'Human Rights'.

Till the nineteenth and the beginning of the twentieth century, any attempt to enforce human rights was considered as an attack upon the concept of State sovereignty. However, there were exceptions like the adoption of the Slavery Convention of 1926 and the establishment of International Labour Organisation in 1919. The huge losses of human life and gross abuses of human rights that took place during World Wars developed the modern human rights instruments. The Covenant of the League of Nations adopted at the end of WWI also included some issues of human rights. The goals of League of Nations included disarmament; preventive war through collective security; settling of disputes between countries through negotiation and diplomacy; and improving global welfare which paves a way towards protection of human rights. Enshrined in its Charter was a mandate to promote many of the rights later included in the Universal Declaration of Human Rights (UDHR).

The realization of the worth of human being led the Institute of International Law to issue a Proclamation of Rights of Man in 1929. Instead of enumerating the rights of human beings, it laid down six duties of the State. The Proclamation of 1929 recognized the right of every individual to life, liberty and prosperity; the rights without any distinction as to nationality, sex, race, language; the right of every individual to the free practice in public or private of any faith, religion or belief. The Proclamation may be regarded as the first attempt towards the universalization of human rights.

The turning point came in the 1940s, in the midst of the extreme abuses of human rights in war-torn Europe during WWII. Atrocious crimes were being committed against humanity and there was a total suppression of fundamental human rights. The Nazi leaders of Germany had established a regime of complete lawless and tyranny. They had barbarously negated all human values and dignity within the territories under their occupation. It was at this time the restoration of the freedom and rights of the people was accepted as one of the essential condition for the establishment of international peace and security. The spirit of this principle was well reflected in the Proclamation issued by the American President Franklin D. Roosevelt on 1941, which came to be known as 'Four Freedoms' which includes freedom of speech, freedom of religion, freedom from want and freedom from fear. In his message Roosevelt declared that freedom means the supremacy of human rights everywhere. (Jones & Myers, 1940-41) In the Moscow Declaration of German Atrocities of 1943, the United States, the United Kingdom, France and the Soviet Union declared that the Germans should be held responsible individually for their violation of international law. A number of conferences and meetings were held before the formation of the United Nations as an international organization in 1945. These include: United Nations Declaration, 1942; Moscow Declaration, 1943; Tehran Declaration, 1943; Dumbarton Oaks Conference, 1944; Yalta Conference, 1945 and San Francisco Conference, 1945. A joint declaration was issued by President Franklin D. Roosevelt of the United States and Prime Minister Winston Churchill of the United Kingdom in 1941 in a document known as 'the Atlantic Charter'. The declaration of the United Nations was signed in 1942 was the first document which used the term human rights. (Agarwal, 2002) In this document the signatories who were fighting against Axis Powers recognised the need to "preserve human rights and justice in their own land as well as other lands". (1942: Declaration of the United Nations)

UN and Human Rights

The Charter of UN represents a significant advancement in the direction of faith and respect for human rights. The appalling atrocities perpetrated by the Nazis against the Jews and other races during WWII led to a strong movement towards international protection of fundamental human rights. The delegates from some countries at the San Francisco Conference were in favour of the adoption of even stronger provision concerning human rights. An unsuccessful attempt to incorporate an International Bill on Human Rights was also made in the UN Charter. Still one can find concern for the promotion of human rights and fundamental freedoms in the Preamble and in Articles 1, 13(b), 55, 56, 62(2), 68 and 76(c).

Since the UN Charter did not contain a chapter on human rights, an attempt was made by drawing up the 'Universal Declaration of Human Rights'. With a view to achieve this, the General Assembly of the UN requested the Economic and Social Council to get a report on the purpose from the Commission on Human Rights. The Commission under the chairmanship of Franklin Roosevelt began work in 1947, appointed a Drafting Committee for preparing Universal Declaration of Human Rights. General Assembly adopted the drafting finalized by the Commission in 1948. Rights for all members of the human family were first articulated here and its thirty articles together form a comprehensive statement covering economic, social, political and cultural and civil rights. This Declaration is both universal since it applies to all people everywhere and indivisible since all rights are equally important to the full realization of one's humanity.

Although the Universal Declaration has achieved the status of customary international law in its nearly seventy years journey as a declaration, it is only a statement of intent, set of principles to which UN member states commit themselves in an effort to provide all people a life of human dignity. For the rights defined in a declaration to have full legal force, they must be written into documents called conventions or covenants, which set international norms and standards.

Immediately after the Universal Declaration was adopted by the UN, work began to codify the rights it contained into legally binding conventions. For political and procedural reasons, these rights were divided between two separate covenants, each addressing different categories of rights. The International Covenant on Civil and Political Rights (ICCPR) articulates the specific, liberty-oriented rights that a state may not take from its citizens, such as freedom of expression and freedom of movement. The International Covenant on Economic, Social and Cultural Rights (ICESCR) addresses those articles in the Declaration that define an individual's rights to self-determination as well as basic necessities, such as food, housing and health care, which a state should provide for its citizen. The UNGA adopted both the covenants in 1966 which came into force in 1976 after the requisite number of States ratified them.

Since its adoption in 1948, the Universal Declaration has served as the foundation for nearly twenty major human rights conventions. Together these constitute the Human Rights Framework, the evolving body of these international documents that define human rights and establish mechanisms to promote and protect them.

Principal United Nations Conventions on Human Rights

- Convention on the Prevention and Punishment of the Crime of Genocide, 1948
- Convention Relating to the Status of Refugees, 1951.
- Slavery Convention of 1926, Amended by Protocol, 1953.
- International Covenant on Civil and Political Rights, 1966.
- International Convention on the Elimination of all forms of Racial Discrimination, 1966.
- Convention on the Non-applicability of Statutory Limitations to War Crimes and Crimes against Humanity, 1968.

- Convention on the Elimination of all forms of Discrimination against Women 1979.
- Convention against Torture and other Cruel, Inhuman or Degrading Treatment or Punishment, 1984.
- Convention on the Rights of the Child, 1989.
- Convention on the Rights of Migrant Workers and the Members of their Families, 1990.
- Convention on the Rights of Persons with Disabilities, 2006.

Human Rights Framework is dynamic. As needs for certain groups of people are recognized and defined and as world events point to the need of awareness and action on specific human rights issues, international human rights law continuously evolves in response. For example, when the Universal Declaration was written in 1948, few people recognized the danger of environmental degradation; therefore this document does not mention environment. At the beginning of the twentieth century, however, activists and governments are working to draft a new convention linking human rights to a safe and healthy environment.

Today many human rights conventions have entered into force as international law; some still in the process of ratification. Others, such as a convention on the rights of indigenous peoples and a convention on environmental rights, are currently being drafted through collaborative efforts of governments and non-governmental organizations (NGO). Since the founding of the UN the role of NGOs has grown steadily. Today it is the NGOs, large and small, local and international that carries the voices and concerns of the ordinary people to the UN.

Like all human endeavour, the UN and the Human Rights Framework that has evolved under its auspices is imperfect. Many critics say the world does not need more human rights conventions but instead the full implementation of those already established. Others believe that the UN system is so flawed that the high ideals and standard it seeks to establish lack credibility. However, in the scope of human history, both the UN and Human Rights Framework are in their infancy. The challenge to citizens of all countries is to work towards evolving more effective UN institution without compromising the high ideals on which the UN is founded.

References

Agarwal, H. (2002). *International Law and Human Rights.* Allahabad: Central Law Publications.

Ahamadi, J. A. (2000). *Inaugural Address on Fakhruddin Ali Ahamed Memorial Lecture on Democracy, Liberty and Changing Political Scenario.* New Delhi : GHAL B. Institute Publication.

Barsan, C. (2005). *The European Convention of Human Rights, Vol. 1, Rights and Liberties, AllBeck, Bucharest.* Bucharest: All Beck.

Blackstone, W. (1765). *The Commentaries on the Laws of England.* London: Clarendon Press.

Closca, I. Ion Suceava. (1995). *Treaty of Human Rights, .* Bucharest: Europa Nova.

Desai, A. R. (1991). *Expanding Governmental Lawlessness and Organised Struggles.* Bombay: Popular Prakashan.

Dicey, A. V. (1885). *Introduction to the Study of the Law of the Constitution.* New York: Macmillan & Co.

Giriraj Shah, K. G. (2001). *Human Rights: Free and Equal.* New Delhi: Anmol Publications.

Jones, S. S., & Myers, D. P. (1940-41). *Documents on American Foreign Relations.* Boston: World Peace Foundation.

Kumar, V. (2003). *Human Rights: Dimension and Issues.* New Delhi: Anmol Publications.

Marcus Tullius Cicero, Niall Rudd, J.G.F. Powell. (1998). *Cicero: The Republic and the Laws.* Oxford: Oxford University Press.

Miller, F. D. (1995). *Nature, Justice and Rights in Aristotle's Politics.* Oxford: Oxford University Press.

Montesquieu, C. L. (2005). *De l'esprit de lex .* Bucharest: Stiintifica.

Nina Redman, Lucille Whalen. (1998). *Human Rights: A Reference Handbook.* Santa Barbara, CA: ABC-CLIO.

Parekh, P. H. (2010). *Human Rights Yearbook, 2010.* Gurgaon: Universal Law Publishing.

Rousseau, J. (1762). *The Social Contract.* Amsterdam: Chez Marc Michel Rey.

Wines, W. A. (2006). *Ethics, Law and Business.* Hove: Psychology Press.

1942: Declaration of the United Nations. (n.d.). Retrieved June 28, 2018, from United Nations: http://www.un.org/en/sections/history-united-nations-charter/1942-declaration-united-nations/index.html

Chapter - II

Identity, Culture and Human Rights: The Universality-Difference Debate

— *Molly Ghosh*

Introduction

The idea of Human Rights is presently very commonly used and frequently referred to by the policy makers, the citizens, various organs of the state, different international agencies and the media either to protest or to justify different policies and activities. Human Rights today is not mere a concept, it has become an agenda of new social movements. The Human Rights movement with its several complexities and diversities has emerged as a transnational social and political movement. Human Rights, as it is commonly understood today, has an underlying idea of universality in the sense that certain rights are enumerated as suitable for everyone irrespective of any context. It is at this point that the question of identity and culture comes in and we find a crucial point of departure from the universality principle of Human Rights. Identity rights and cultural rights demand that rights should be culturally contextual rather than having the paradigm of universality. They focus on difference and particularity rather than universality. In the post Cold War world multicultural societies, voluntary migration of people and open market economy made culture and identity important issues. In global politics, culture became an important organising principle and cultural dimension of Human Rights focusing on identity became as crucial as the civil, political, social and economic ones. Human Rights have been a debatable issue always regarding definition of rights, the ideology behind the rights, the cultural context of rights, entitlements of rights and the process of implementation of rights. To understand the point of debate we need to examine the politics of Human Rights and develop an understanding of different theoretical positions of Human Rights.

Contemporary Definition of Human Rights

The history of Human Rights needs to be examined to understand its contemporary definition. According to a particular perspective, the concept of Human Rights has no historical roots of origin and it was entirely a post World War II development and an innovation of the United Nations (UN). From this perspective, the Universal Declaration of Human Rights (UDHR), made by the United Nations is the origin of the concept. Whether we accept the claim that Human Rights have little or no history before the United Nations, it is a fact that the contemporary idea of Human Rights is based upon the Universal Declaration of Human Rights, 1948. It has a legal perspective and mostly understood as a legal doctrine. With its claim of universality, it was more related with the idea of International Law rather than domestic law. International Law, since the inception of the idea, has been exclusively concerned with sovereignty of States, their actions in the international arena and regulation of relations between States so that they refrain from interfering in each other's internal affairs. The objective was ensuring international peace. It was with the UDHR that the UN introduced the legal idea of regulating the relations between the State and the individual. The idea was launched without any interference with the sovereignty of the States and the latter was given the responsibility to execute the rights. The concept of Human Rights became an essential part of the discourse of the allied forces in the World War II since 1941. The then United States President Roosevelt presented his vision of a post World War II world based on 'four essential human freedoms': freedom of speech and expression, freedom of worship, freedom from want and freedom from fear. He equated freedom as supremacy of Human Rights everywhere. President Roosevelt mentioned this idea of freedom on 6 January 1941 in his annual State of the Union address to the Congress. Later British Prime Minister, Winston Churchill, also shared the same view and together they made an eight point declaration that came to be known as the Atlantic Charter. The Charter set out some common aims of which there was establishment of peace and guarantee of Human Rights and justice. The formation of the UN was an Allied forces endeavour and through the Declaration of UN in 1942 the Allied forces asserted that to protect the future world from gross Human Rights abuse like the Nazi anti-Semitic atrocities, it is required to preserve Human Rights and justice and only their victory in the war can ensure this. The Charter of the UN declared that one of the chief aims of the organization is 'to reaffirm faith in fundamental human rights, in the dignity and worth of the human person, in the equal rights of men and women and of nations large and small'. The UN was established to support the world vision of the Allied forces, which were mostly liberal democratic states. The objective was to establish a new world order based on liberal principles. The entire course of evolution of UDHR was political as it was evolved as an essential part of the Western liberal world view. The UDHR has an individualistic orientation as the rights ensured were primarily individual rights and with this document individual needs and interests became an issue of global politics. The idea of Human Rights propounded through the UN was Western but it was given a global perspective. The rights that were primarily ensured in the doctrine were compatible with the liberal principles. This

Western model of Human Rights dominated the post World War II discourse on rights.

The UDHR was formed as a legal document and the idea of Human Rights that propagated through the UDHR has a legal perspective. The signatory States of UDHR were expected to incorporate the rights through their respective constitutional frameworks and take other necessary measures to ensure the rights. Formation of structural frameworks like committees and commissions at the international and domestic levels followed to execute the UDHR. The field of Human Rights became a technical and legal discourse with lawyers dominating it and law seemed to provide the objective standards that would make the concept secured from moral and political controversies. (Freeman, 2011)

The Philosophical Roots

Human Rights in the UDHR were defined as rights to which people are entitled by virtue of being human and they were claimed as universal in the sense that they belong to human beings globally irrespective of race, religion, gender and other differences. The philosophical roots of the concept lied in the moral doctrine that human beings have an intrinsic worth and dignity and they can never be deprived of that worth. The role of the State is to ensure that dignity. The Western idea of Human Rights has its philosophical origin in the concept of Roman jurisprudence and its idea of Natural Rights. The origin of Natural Rights was in the Roman idea of *jus naturale*. The first formulation of a concept of Natural Rights took place in the philosophy of late Middle Ages. But the idea of Natural Rights has never emerged as something inevitable or universally acceptable even in Western thought. There have always existed other alternatives. Plato has discussed an ideal state and society without any conception of Natural Rights. But in some other Greek philosophers we find the conception of rights in the form of protection of individuals against abuse of power by the State. The idea of Natural Law was elaborated by the Stoics who have based it upon the Aristotelian idea of nature. The Stoic tradition was later continued by the Christian tradition of thought reflected through St. Thomas Aquinas. Scholars differ in their views on whether Greek philosophy has a language of rights. MacIntyre argued that there was never any language of right in ancient Greek thought. (MacIntyre, 1981) His views were rejected by others who argued that Aristotle has imbibed an idea of rights as he said that Constitutions could assign rights to citizens. Similar ambiguity is there in Christian thought also. Moses gave commandments to the children of Israel not a code of rights. The Christian church has suppressed rights in some contexts but affirmed them in others. (Tierney, 2004) The idea of rights was there but it was not universal. It was in twelfth century that through the juristic concept of *jus naturale* the idea of natural rights got its shape. Michael Villey has initiated a debate on the distinction between subjective rights and objective rights. He argued that early Roman Law had no conception of subjective rights as rights were not viewed as personal entitlements. They were rather objective rights or about the right order of society. Duties were of more importance than rights. They were held as important for limiting the realm of desire and help man remove his moral perplexities. In its origin, natural rights were not rights of individual. The older doctrine on Natural Rights imposed obligations on the citizens for the sake of right order of society but the modern conception focused on self-assertion of individuals. The shift from objective rights to subjective rights took place in late Middle ages and with the change from medieval to modern era the idea of duty gave way to the idea of right. Villey argued that the doctrine of subjective rights was first evolved by the fourteenth century Francisian philosopher, William of Ockham. Ockham's nominalist philosophy always asserted that only individual entities have real existence. (Tierney, 2004)

The modern conception of Human Rights is highly indebted to the Lockean idea of Natural Rights though it is often argued that Hobbes was first to produce a notion of natural rights. He defends an idea of right over one's own and one another's body, which man renounces once he gives his consent to form a sovereign. He relinquishes his right to the sovereign established through a contract. Lockean views asserted a right of resistance to any sort of unjust authority. He was particularly concerned with how individuals can have right to their property. Though in his earlier works Locke has often held a different argument on political obedience, in his *Two Treatises of Government* he questioned the ground of obligation to absolute power of the monarchy and defends a right of active disobedience to protect one's own life, liberty and property. He argues that these are rights which are based upon the Christian conception of the law of nature. All human rights and human duties are derived from the law of nature and knowledge of the law of nature is compulsive for all men. This law of nature is the traditional Christian conception of law of nature wherein political rights and political duties are all derived from God's will. The idea of universalism was inherent in this tradition of natural law.

If the history of development of Natural Rights from Middle age to modern age is studied we will find that there was a debate on the question that whether claims to natural rights are exclusively for Western culture or all people are entitled to have such rights. A particular historic event changed the course of Human Rights thinking and it was the Spanish conquest of America. The incident raised a debate among Spanish scholars that whether aboriginal American Indians have any rights. Those who justified the conquest denied any conception of rights of native Americans while those who opposed the position argued that the native Americans were in all respect humans and entitled to have land and self government.

The idea of Human Rights with its ancient roots has always been associated with diverse religion and philosophies of the world. An idea of rights was even found in the Codes of Hammurabi. Conceived as one of the oldest code of laws of the ancient world, the pre-biblical Codes of Hammurabi was a compendium of 282 laws covering diverse aspects of individuals' lives like property, criminal justice and family. The concept of rights was there in the codes as reflected through the laws. The edicts of King Ashoka is also said to have comprising the idea of rights of citizens. The idea of rights has diverse philosophical roots and the Christian tradition of thought is only one of them. With Hobbes or Locke it became attached with the ideology of liberalism but with an individualist orientation and after the Second World War codified and deployed strategically in a global context as a liberal idea. The doctrine of universalist liberalism became the basis of the idea of Natural Rights and subsequently Human Rights were also conceived as something universal with a focus on the individual. The individualism of seventeenth and eighteenth centuries that was associated with Natural Rights was percolated to Human Rights also.

The Debate

The idea of Human Rights and the universalist assumptions underlying the idea was challenged particularly since 1970s giving rise to a debate between universalism and difference or an emphasis on the question of cultural relativism. The debate became increasingly relevant after the dissolution of USSR and the onset of globalization. The global movement of labour created multicultural societies with every State having a more diverse diaspora with diverse cultures. It became increasingly difficult to codify universal principles of rights on issues of cultural practices like female genital mutilation or *hijab*. Philosophically, the idea of Human Rights, as it was conceived by the Western Liberal School was challenged by two main philosophical developments – communitarianism and post-modernism.

Liberal vision of politics have never included any independent principle of community such as shared nationality, language, identity, culture, religion, history or way of life. (Kymlicka, 2005) Communitarianism challenged the basic liberal assumption of asocial, atomized and 'unencumbered self' and questioned the primacy of individual over community. Communitarians conceived the individual self as embedded in a community and the individual as a mere reflection of the broader community (Sandel, 1982) & (Taylor, 1992). From this perspective there can be never any universal concept of justice and rights as the liberals claim. An individual is the embodiment of the society to which he belongs and his needs are shaped by his social context. He cannot have any right out of that social context. Rights should be local, particular and contextual, having relation to the community to which the individual belongs. Rather than universality, difference should be the principle. They argue for replacing or at least supplementing the liberal politics of right with a politics of common good. Rights should be determined not by the individual but in terms of common good. They challenge the individualist liberal conception of the right to self-determination of individuals on the ground that the liberals misconstrue an individual's capacity for self-determination and neglect the social preconditions under which that capacity can be meaningfully exercised. (Kymlicka, 2005)

Postmodernism, in its critique of the thrust on universalism through the 'Enlightenment Project', has put forth a similar view regarding universal concept of rights. Enlightenment called for universalizing the world in terms defined by the West. It was all about establishing the politico-cultural hegemony of the West on the rest of the world. Postmodernism questions this model. It also argues for particularity and difference. It conceived Human Rights as another metanarrative of modernity and calls for using it with modifications based on the political and cultural context. With its approach of 'incredulity towards metanarratives', Postmodernism questions liberalism itself and any idea, that reflects the liberal worldview. There can never be any objective model of Human Rights. Neither can there be any universal model of Human Rights. The question of cultural relativism in Human Rights was also raised by the postcolonial critiques who argued that the concept of Human Rights is not exclusively a Western idea and there are alternative ideas of Human Rights. They held universal Human Rights as nothing but a sort of cultural imperialism of the West. Cultural context is different for different societies and so there can never be any objective universal model of Human Rights.

Scholars supporting cultural relativism argue that there is always a necessary tension between relativity and universality. Radical universalism always implies a moral imperialism whereby the moral standards of a particular culture come to dominate over others. Donnelly defines radical universalism as a position opposite to radical cultural relativism. While radical cultural relativism holds that culture is the sole source of validity of any moral right or rule, radical universalism argue that culture is irrelevant for the validity of any moral rights or rule. Moral rules like Human Rights function within a broad moral community and radical universalism is based on a hierarchical order of moral communities whereby some communities are placed on a higher order than others. Cosmopolitan moral communities are given priority over other ones. Cultural relativists raise objections on three main grounds. (Donnelly, 1984) The first one is regarding the substance of the list of Human Rights. They claim that there cannot be any substantive list of Human Rights like the UDHR or other international covenants. The list of Human Rights should be culturally determined and there must exist some allowances for the special practices of national or other non-cosmopolitan moral communities. The second objection is regarding the interpretation of Human Rights. Interpretation of Human Rights is also culturally-determined. The perception of what constitutes violation is not necessarily the same in all societies. The third objection is regarding the form in which Human Rights are implemented in different societies.

During 1980s and 1990s an idea emerged that Asian values, culture and beliefs can well form an alternative to

Western values that are having global dominance. This challenge to the Western hegemony in matters of Human Rights became evident clearly in the Bangkok Declaration of 1993. Representatives of Asian states, who met to prepare for the World Conference on Human Rights in Vienna, were signatories of this declaration. Through this declaration a statement was made in favour of Asian values and challenging Western values in the realm of Human Rights. The issue of difference and cultural relevance was reflected in a global forum. The advocates of Asian values argued that Human Rights have always been based on West-defined assumptions that gave primacy of individual over community and rights over duty. An alternative perspective based on Asian values has the potential to change this and usher in a better concept of Human Rights. An alternative to UDHR was also provided by the Cairo Declaration on Human Rights in Islam (1990). It challenged the UDHR as a cultural expression of economic and political domination of the Western hegemony. It argued for a framework of Human Rights in congruence with *Sharia* Law for the Islamic world. The World Conference on Human Rights in Vienna (1993) adopted the Vienna Declaration and Programme of Action. Welcoming the International Year of World's Indigenous People in 1993, it reaffirmed the commitment of the International community to ensure enjoyment of all Human Rights and fundamental freedom by indigenous people and to respect the value and diversity of their cultures and identities. As a part of the programme of action it was asserted that the significance of national and regional particularities and various historical, cultural and religious backgrounds must be borne in mind (Vienna Declaration and Programme of Action: Adopted by the World Conference on Human Rights in Vienna on 25 June 1993, 2018). The Vienna Declaration also emphasized the rights of particular groups like women, children, disabled persons, refugees and migrant workers. The Vienna Declaration can be said to be a response of the UN to the critique of universalism.

Conclusion

Human Rights, presently understood as a legal document, have a rich philosophical lineage. Its lineage is concerned with Natural Law, human nature and morality with philosophers from a wide spectrum and diverse traditions of thought having their views on it. Human Rights is not merely a legal text, it should always be supplemented by economics, politics and moral philosophy. In its evolution it came to be associated with the liberal worldview and took on the perspective of universalism and we cannot deny that through the idea of universalism the moral standards of a particular community dominated over others. The challenge came from different perspectives but all of them were critical of the domination of Western liberal worldview. The contemporary world with its rich diversities, active assertion of self-determination, politicipation of identity and culture issues have made the course of formulation, interpretation and implementation of Human Rights complicated. Rights of individuals come in conflict with self-determination of communities. Universal Human Rights often contradicts the moral standards of smaller communities. On the contrary, if we use the idea of Human Rights we have to agree on a point that there is something basic of being a human and therein come again the question of universality. Universal Human Rights with some due importance to difference and particularity seems a logical impossibility. The present Human Rights regime is adopting a path of accommodation with allowances to ethnic, religious or linguistic minorities. But a more serious thinking on the entire process of Human Rights needs to be developed to make the regime of rights robust and effective.

References

Donnelly, J. (1984). Cultural Relativism and Universal Human Rights. *Human Rights Quaterly*, 400-419.

Freeman, M. (2011). *Human Rights An Interdisciplinary Approach.* Cambridge: Polity Press.

Kymlicka, W. (2005). *Contemporary Political Philosophy.* New Delhi: Oxford University Press.

MacIntyre, M. (1981). *After Virtue.* Notre Dame: University of Notre Dame Press.

Sandel, M. (1982). *Liberalism and the Limits of Justice.* Cambridge: Cambridge University Press.

Taylor, C. (1992). The Politics of Recognition In A. Gutman, *Multiculturalism and 'Politics of Recognition'* (pp. 25-73). Princeton: Princeton University Press.

Tierney, B. (2004). The Idea of Natural Rights:Origin and Persistence. *Northwestern Journal of International Human Rights*, 2-12.

Vienna Declaration and Programme of Action: Adopted by the World Conference on Human Rights in Vienna on 25 June 1993. (2018). Retrieved March 31, 2018, from United Nations Human Rights Office of the High Commissioner: https://www.ohchr.org/EN/ProfessionalInterest/Pages/Vienna.aspx

Chapter - III

Gender and Entrepreneurship in India: A Right Based Perspective & Ground Reality

— *Chandan Roy and Susmita Chatterjee*

Introduction

"A power of fallen boundless self awake........
.......Her body of glory expunged from heaven
The rarity and wonder lived no more."

Savitri, Sri Aurobindo

One day, the 'oppressed -sex' will rise from the obscurity with glory and the power will be recognised through the social exercise. The domain of study of 'gender and entrepreneurship' emphasises on the nature and transformation of leadership qualities of the weaker gender in the business world, which is governed by the rules and rights of patriarchy. Being socio-economic phenomenon, entrepreneurship is again dependent on cultural framework of the society and the consequent constitutional right and protection the society confers to its weaker sex. In paradigm of Economics, entrepreneurial action is a model of social interaction which hinges upon the initiative taking and zeal of the entrepreneurs and also on their risk taking attitude. The symbolic meaning of 'enterprise' is encapsulated by few traits of the entrepreneurs, which includes qualities like, astute, pragmatic, imaginative, open-minded and audacious. Thus, they resided in the symbolic domain of the male patriarchy for a long period until the process of globalization and liberalization started. The symbolic order of gender used to assign the sphere of activity and pro-activity to the male, while it associated passivity, adaptation and flexibility with the female. In a culture, however, the symbolic gender order is not absolute: it is not static but dynamic and therefore varies across time and space. The meaning of 'gender', as it is historically and culturally situated, lies in its deferral by gender relationships (Gherardi, 1995) & (S. Gherardi, B. Poggio, 2003) and also influenced by the country's constitutional rules and rights.

This paper will unravel different right-based dimensions of gendered entrepreneurship in India and would elaborate the hardcore reality the women entrepreneurs are facing right now, despite provisions of those rights and protection. Eventually we would justify the dire need of female enterprise in our socio-political and cultural space while contextualising the issue in economic perspective. In short, the major objective of this paper is to locate the gender based dimension of entrepreneurship in Indian economy against its right based perspective and to measure the gap and explain the lacunae behind this difference. The following sections would sequentially clarify these issues. The second section will illustrate the constitutional provisions of women entrepreneurs as guaranteed by Indian constitution. The third section will elaborate the actual scenario of women entrepreneurs in Indian economy and would assess their strengths and weaknesses. The fourth section will try to reason out the gap between actual and ideal position of women entrepreneurs, especially from the rights based perspective, while the concluding section will summarise the whole analysis and suggest some way ahead.

Right Based Standpoint of Gender & Entrepreneurship in India

Entrepreneurship as a cultural practice rests upon activities that are founded on embodied understanding and constitutional background. The symbolic representation is rooted directly in the gendered body, too. Consequently, a gender analysis of entrepreneurship differs from an analysis of women entrepreneurs because it examines the way in which gender is culturally constructed by these social practices that constitute the social phenomenon of entrepreneurship. Our objective in this section is to locate the constitutional rights and protection of the working women, while contextualising them in the arena of 'gender and entrepreneurship'. In India, the Preamble of the Constitution unequivocally declares equality of status and opportunity of all its citizens irrespective of their sex. A number of Fundamental Rights guaranteed to the individuals in Part III of the Indian Constitution are similar to the provisions of the Universal Declaration of Human Rights. These include the Right to Equality, Right to Freedom, Right against Exploitation, Right to Freedom of Religion, Cultural Educational Rights and Right to Constitutional remedies. These Fundamental Rights will be applicable irrespective of sexes. Article 14 proclaims the general right of all persons to equality before the law, while Article 15 prohibits the State from discriminating against any citizen on grounds of religion, race, caste, sex or place of birth, and prohibits any restriction on any citizen's access to any public place. Equality of opportunity for all citizens in matters of public employment is guaranteed under Article 16, which reconfirms the equal rights of the women in work space.

The right to freedom guaranteed to all citizens under Article 19 encompasses the right to freedom of speech and expression, the right to assemble peaceably without arms, the right to form associations or unions, the right to move freely throughout the territory of India, the right of residence, and the right to practice any profession, or to carry on any occupation, trade or business. Thus the Fundamental Rights provides the ability to all citizens of the country to open his/her enterprise within geographical territory of the country.

On the other hand, Directive Principles of State Policy in Part-IV of the Indian constitution offers equal opportunity for both men and women in matter of public employment and equal pay for equal jobs. The duties of the State encompass securing a social order with justice, social, economic and political, striving to minimize and eliminate all inequalities (Article 38), securing for the citizens, men and women equally, the right to an adequate means of livelihood (Article 39 (a)),distribution of ownership and control of community resources to subserve the common good (Article 39(b)), securing equal pay for equal work for both men and women (Article 39(d)), preventing abuse of labour, provision of the right to work, education and public assistance in case of unemployment, provision of humane conditions of work (Article 42), living wage and a decent standard of life (Article 43), securing participation of workers in the management of industries (Article 43A).

To focus attention on women entrepreneurs from ethnographic standpoint, contributes to their continual othering, where 'othering' refers to the process through which a dominant group overpowers an inferior group. Socio-economic studies – by means of analysis of statistics on labour-market participation – tell us that the phenomenon differed qualitatively from a simple expansionary trend. (Barbieri, 1999) For example, in Italy during the 1990s, self-employment by women was no longer a 'fall-back solution' except in a very small number of cases. (Zanfrini, 1999) Barbieri (1999) also points out that a distinctive feature of the 1990s was the specialization and differentiation of occupations and sectors of activity. Those years saw increased numbers of women working in the professions, as partners in cooperatives, in business services and social services; but their numbers declined or were stationary in traditional activities and services like retail and small-scale commerce, or in the traditional manufacturing sectors in which women work as 'helpers' for other members of the family. Consequently, female entrepreneurship is now growing in sectors where there is space for professional growth and demand for specialist skills, and it is declining in the traditional and low-skilled sectors. These features are not exclusive to Italy but seem to be shared by the European countries and also by the United States (Barbieri, 1999).

Premises on Entrepreneurship & Gender

Entrepreneurial action is considered in terms of its cultural dimension, the processes by which value is attributed to its various components (for example, risk, money and innovativeness), and the ways in which entrepreneurship is socially represented in the discursive practices with which subjects describe, explain and legitimate to themselves and others what they do when they 'do entrepreneurship'.

Our assumptions on gender pertain to what is known as 'social constructionism' (Gergen, 1982), and therefore gender is defined as 'the gender we think and the gender we do'. (Gherardi, 1994) This approach follows in the tradition of studying gender dynamics as an active accomplishment (West, Zimmerman, 1987), as performativity (Butler, 1993), as a two-sided dynamic of gendering practices and practising of gender. (Martin, 1993) Gender is the historico-material product of 'positioning' practices. (Gherardi, 2003) Although the concept of gender includes male, female and gender non-binary people, but this study would be limited within the gender binary categorization.

Premises On Change In Gender Relations

All the social sciences are reflexive (Giddens, 1979) in that they change the phenomena that they analyse, but studies on gender – judging from the magnitude of the changes that have come about in the last thirty-odd years – have had an especial impact on society. The most pervasive of them, we believe, although it has been less thematized as such, is the crisis of hegemonic masculinity. (Connell, 1995) The destabilization of gender categories and gender relations is a pervasive social phenomenon that traverses the boundaries between spheres – public/private, family/work or inside/outside the firm – where they were previously kept separate.

In a private multi-person household, marriage is an institution which binds two persons in familial relation. In a society, in which people choose to stay in marital/living relation, depends upon their perceptions about future benefits and costs. In a family dyad much of the power generation and transfer depend upon the source of capital and income generating factors. A woman would be known as 'true entrepreneur' of her family business, if she has the ability to take independent decisions.

Work-participation in labour force has also expanded throughout the world. Women have started getting access both traditionally female and male occupation. Blue collar occupations remain the most heavily male area of the occupation, which include production jobs, craft jobs such as carpenters and electricians, the transportation related jobs as well as less skilled jobs such as garbage collectors and construction labourers. On the other hand, most of the pink collar jobs, like clerical and service occupations were feminized by 1970 and continued their process of feminization till now. Meanwhile men continued to shun these jobs. Only three service occupations had noticeable gains in male representation e.g., cooks, kitchen workers and house workers. In several professions like lawyer, doctors, chartered accountants, actors, tutors, playing coaches trends of rising female participation is noticeable across the world. Female lawyers are supposed to be having greatest impact on the law professions as well as on the working world. Their efforts to redraw the landscape of the legal world by replacing the 'male' value system of Rights, Rules and Hierarchies with female value based Rights and Responsibilities. The Rights based perspectives have been reinforced with more and more representation of women in judicial as well as political arena.

UN Working Group on Discrimination against Women in Law and Practice has stated in their background paper (2014) that business around the world has been growing during the last few decades though women remain almost excluded in the top echelon of business decision makers. However, competition has led the big business houses to outsource work to other parts of the world with cheaper unskilled labour, where women are concentrated in global value chains. According to ILO (2011), sex based discrimination remain the most prevalent form of inequality in work area, which hinders women participation in workforce as well as in business decision making avenues.

Trends of Women Entrepreneurship in India: Assessing Strength & Weaknesses

Till 1850, manufacturing entrepreneurship did not exist in India due to weak communication and transportation systems of the colonial political structure. The British rulers might indirectly ignite some male entrepreneurship, while women entrepreneurship was hardly possible. The year 1850 was earmarked as introduction of modern factory system in India, as the first cotton mill was set up in Bombay (now Mumbai) by a Parsi. In 1907, J.N. Tata started iron and steel industry and thus Parsis dominated the entrepreneurship domain in the first wave of entrepreneurship.

The second wave of entrepreneurial growth began after the First World War. During these decades,-cement and sugar industries experienced fast progress. Along with that the relative importance of Parsis declined and the Gujrati and Marwari and Vaishyas emerged. The preconditions for innovating entrepreneurship had come into existence but the managerial talents still lacked. After the Second World War, the process of entrepreneurial growth got momentum. At that period, Indian economy has been undergoing through rapid change. During the war, Government of India helped the entrepreneurs to give boost to the growth rate of industries and entrepreneurs earned high profits. But soon after the war, the production went below average, and the entrepreneurs experienced a setback. However, one thing is very prominent women entrepreneurship was not at all prominent during that phase. During the Pre-Independence days, no concrete public or private financial and non-financial support systems were available to foster entrepreneurship.

In the Post Independence periods, several Industrial Policies were introduced for fostering Entrepreneurship. The Government nationalized the banks and set up state financial corporation along with designing various income generating schemes to reach out to the women entrepreneurs. Post liberalization, various private support bodies specifically for women entrepreneurs, like TIE The Indus Entrepreneurs with their TiE Stree Shakti, NEN (National Entrepreneurship Network) through its Goldman Sachs 1000 women entrepreneurs Program and Federation of Indian Women Entrepreneurs (FIWE) have supported 60% of the women entrepreneurs of the total sample in terms of technical guidance. All the women Entrepreneurs have received physical support from their family members. 85% of the respondents have received funding from their family members. Some of the support systems which supported the women entrepreneurs over the period are as listed in Table 3.1.

Table 3.1: Support Systems of Women Entrepreneurship In India

Institutions	*Year*
Central Bank of India Credit Schemes	1911
Self-Employment Women's Association	1972
National Bank for Agriculture and Rural Development (NABARD)	1982
State Government Schemes for Development of Women and Children in Rural Areas (DWCRA)	1982
Association of Women Entrepreneurs of Karnataka (AWAKE)	1983
Small Industries Development Bank of India (SIDBI)	1990
Federation of Indian Women Entrepreneurs (FIWE)	1993

(*Contd...*)

Consortium of Women Entrepreneurship in India (CWEI)	1996
The Indus Entrepreneurs- Stree Shakti	2009
National Entrepreneurship Network-Goldman Sachs 1000 Women Entrepreneurs	2009
Google India Women on Web	2012

Source: Lal (2012)

At the advent of Independence the Government of India tried to focus in Industrialization with specific interest to large scale industries in coordination with the Government. It was in the 1977 Industrial Policy Resolution, the Government focused on Entrepreneurship and Directorate of Industries were set in the districts of the country and allocated Industrial Area for small and medium scale Enterprises. Still there was no significant number of women entrepreneurs. Men themselves were not willing to start their business as according to Hinduism and it was divided earlier into caste system. So, the entrepreneurs were from Vaishya Community (Trading community). People from other community came forward because of compelling reasons. At the same time the representation from the Women Entrepreneurs was abysmally low. Only a handful of women entrepreneurs came forward in reality and became nominal heads of their enterprises and the real business were run by the head of the family like, Father/ Son/ Husband. The number of women Entrepreneurs increased, especially during the 1990s because of Liberalization and New Industrial Policy of 1991 was specially designed to propagate entrepreneurship and boosted Women Entrepreneurs via provisions of several subsidies and allocating quotas. During Liberalization period (i.e., from 1980s to 1990s) the percentage of women entrepreneurs increased from 8.25% to 9.85% and that has further grown to 11.29 in 1990-93. The percentage of women showed a remarkable growth in the tune of 25% in 1993-94, which sustained in 1994-95, though, the percentage of women entrepreneurs happened to be only to be only 13%, on the basis of total number of Entrepreneurs (National Institute of Entrepreneurship and Small Business Development-NIESBUD Report 1992).

Since September, 2008 the industrialized world has undergone a recession, a pronounced declaration of economic activity. This global recession has resulted in a sharp drop in international trade, rising unemployment and slumping commodity prices in December 2008. The conditions leading up to crises, characterized by an exorbitant rise in asset prices and associated boom in economic demand are considered as a result of the extended period of available credit, inadequate regulation and oversight or increasing inequality.

Globally, venture capital funding had fallen to 71 percent in the fourth quarter of 2008 from a year ago, startups have been forced to fold up as they could not sustain their business and investors cannot fund them any longer. This has actually boosted innovation amongst laid –off engineers, scientists and other highly skilled individuals as many of them have decided to pursue their own ideas. Calling it forced entrepreneurship Mark Cannice Professor of Entrepreneurship at San Francisco said that he was optimistic that the current layoffs would unleash the next wave of creative, thoughtful entrepreneurship. Even in India venture capital funding had dropped by 27 % in the first quarter. Post-recession surveys have revealed that many new start-ups with a new work culture have come up and are there in the business arena to last for long and majority of the old ones sailed through the tempest. So a broad insight into the literature survey concludes that a new wave of entrepreneurship is going to thrive in these turbulent times. Compared to the previous level of women entrepreneurs, majority of them were highly educated and tech savvy and young in age, unmarried and determined to pursue their dreams. This new generation of women-owned enterprises is actively seeking capital for their businesses, using modern technology to find and create a niche market both in domestic as well as export frontiers. They work in a wide range of sectors from trade and services, to tailoring, beauty parlors, printing and many more. However, the involvement of the women entrepreneurs in the production/ manufacturing sector is rather slow.

Table 3.2: Female Entrepreneurs in India During 2000-2010

	Percentage Share of Female Entrepreneurs			*Number of Entrepreneurs (in '000)*					
	2000	***2005-6***	***2010***	***2000***		***2005-6***		***2010***	
				Male	***Female***	***Male***	***Female***	***Male***	***Female***
Entrepreneur with Hired Workers (Establishment)									
Manufacturing	6	6	5	1743	113	2136	148	2542	142
Trade	4	NA	3	1774	76	NA	NA	2728	81
Service	6	8	6	1402	95	1885	158	2762	188
Entrepreneur without Hired Workers (Own Account Enterprises)									
Manufacturing	29	43	46	8637	3448	8275	6129	7591	6542
Trade	6	NA	10	14,210	945	NA	NA	15,693	1770
Service	6	9	8	8623	598	11702	1153	13874	1282

Source: Daymard (2015), Different NSS Records.

Female Entrepreneurship in India is Rising Mostly among the Entrepreneurs without Workers

The number of female entrepreneurs has doubled over the past ten years to about 10 million outside the agricultural sector mostly due to the rise in enterprises without hired workers. Their share rose in all sectors, and women now account nearly half of total entrepreneurs without workers in manufacturing. In services and trade their shares have also grown but remained modest at about 10% of total. Given the often marginal nature of these activities, this can result from lack of wage employment opportunities elsewhere in the Indian economy. Despite solid GDP growth over the past decade only 4million new jobs were created for women between 2000 and 2010, mostly in salaried employment in urban areas, while the female working age population not in school increased by 60 million over the period. The remaining 58 million net new jobs were all taken by men. This suggests that the reason for the rise in female entrepreneurship can be a lack of other employment opportunities. However, not all of the rise in entrepreneurship may be captured by employment data if they work only some part of themonth or year.

The Enterprise Survey, conducted in 73 Round NSS (during July 2015-June 2016) estimated that the number of unincorporated and non-agricultural enterprises in the country during 2015-16 was 6.34 crores, out of which 51.3% reside in rural areas and remaining 48.7% live in urban areas. At all India level, 31% were engaged in manufacturing, 36.3% were in trading and 32.6% were in other services irrespective of their sexes. Uttar Pradesh (14.2%) was reported as the highest number of entrepreneurs followed by West Bengal (13.99%), while West Bengal (17.44%) topped among states with highest share of entrepreneurs in rural sector followed by Uttar Pradesh. In the urban sector, Uttar Pradesh was followed by Tamil Nadu in terms of numbers of entrepreneurs. Still, Uttar Pradesh and West Bengal had almost equal share in numbers of entrepreneurs. Uttar Pradesh had higher number of establishments (enterprise with hired workers) than West Bengal, according to the recent enterprise survey. In the proprietor based entrepreneurship, female enterprises comprises 19% share in all India level, while the highest percentage of female proprietors reside in Telengana (37.3%) followed by West Bengal (32.7%).

At all India level, nearly one fifth of the enterprises were proprietary headed by female entrepreneur. However, the concentration was mainly restricted to the Enterprises without hired workers. This is also known as Own Account Enterprises, where they had 22% across all the sectors. Among establishments (which are comparatively bigger enterprise) share of female entrepreneurs reported to be 4-5% only. It is interesting to note that female proprietor enterprise has a share of 45% among manufacturing enterprises, whereas their share in trading and service sectors are 8.7% and 7.4% respectively.

Table 3.3: Percentage Share of Female Proprietors in Different States of India

	States	*Percent of Female Proprietors*
1.	Telengana	37.3
2.	West Bengal	32.7
3.	Tamil Nadu	26.0
4.	Gujarat	24.9
5.	Andhra Pradesh	24.7
6.	Karnataka	24.4
7.	Kerala	20.8
8.	Jharkhand	19.6
9.	Maharashtra	16.8
10.	Punjab	15.3
	All India	**19.5**

Source: NSS 73, Round Survey.

Table 3.4: Percentage Distribution of Entrepreneurs in Proprietor Ownership During 2015-16

	Enterprise without hired Workers	*Enterprise with Hired Workers*	*All Enterprise*
Male	73.9	89.7	76.4
Female	22.3	4.8	19.5

Source: NSS 73 Round (2015-16)

Table 3.5: Percentage Distribution of Proprietary Entrepreneurship

	Broad Activity Category	*Male*	*Female*
1.	Manufacturing	53.2	45.0
2.	Trade	88.8	8.7
3.	Other Services	84.6	7.4

Source: NSS 73 Round (2015-16)

Contributing Factors

Blanchflower and Oswald (1998) explained that the factors which affect the supply of entrepreneurs are important but poorly understood. Through their analysis, it came up that probability of self employment largely depends upon whether the individual received a handsome inheritance gift as 'start up capital', while their personality measurement score in childhood contributes nothing. A study conducted in India by Krishnamoorthy and Bala Subramani (2014) indicated the motivational dimension like, 'ambition', 'knowledge and skill' and 'independence' as the high impact factors behind entrepreneurial success of the women. In another study, Palaniappan, Ramanigopal and Mani (2012) showed that skill, knowledge and adaptability in business are the main reasons for women to emerge in the business ventures, while lack of training, low education and financial crisis made them lagging behind.

Daymard (2015) stated that entrepreneurship can create new economic opportunities for women and contribute to overall growth and exit from poverty. The potential flexibility in time use from entrepreneurship can also facilitate balancing work and family obligations for women. However, male and female, both entrepreneurs are relatively scarce in India compared to peer countries, and tend to work in small units often outside the formal sector. While many of the barriers to entrepreneurship are common to both genders (access to capital and business networks, adequate training and facilities) female entrepreneurs face gender biases stemming from socioeconomic factors or specific biases in laws such as inheritance laws.

Various studies have indicated factors like 'education', 'labour force participation', 'dependent children', 'population density' as the determinants of women entrepreneurship. (Daymard, 2015); (Kolstad, Wiig, 2013) & (Kobeissi, 2010) Daymard (2015) has stated that share of marginalized population inhibits the chance of women entrepreneurship, while political representation has no impact on female business ownership. The relation between entrepreneurship and education appears to be equivocal. In developing countries, it has been observed to be inversely related, as low education confines the women to have access in formal job market and thus they feel bound to make their fortune at informal markets activating their own entrepreneurial zeal. (M. Minniti, W.Naudé, 2010) Brochaus and Nord (1979) also suggested that workers with low education would avoid the ambience of paid jobs. However, the reverse has also been stated by several commentators that opportunity to management skill as well as access to credit decision widens as the education level of female entrepreneurs rises. (Van der Sluis, Van Praag and Vijverberg, 2005); (Kolstad, Wiig, 2013) & (Parker, Van Praag, 2006) Thus, Right to Education, which was implemented in India since 2010, would definitely expand the pace of female entrepreneurship.

Female labour force participation would rise in any society if the traditional gender stereotypes are being challenged. This workforce participation is positively related with numbers of female entrepreneurship. In time of work, a woman labour acquires skill as well as knowledge about business environment, which induces her to transform her work spirit into potential entrepreneurial skill. Daymard (2015) showed high level of female labour force participation is positively correlated with entrepreneurship without workers in India.

Similarly, number of dependent children raises the intensity of women entrepreneurship in India. Dependent children enable their mothers to work from home, staying closer to them. Work flexibility and time gains obtained from not commuting to external business sector, would allow the women entrepreneurs to strike the balance between family and professional life. (Kobeissi, 2010) Higher population density also expands the opportunity of female entrepreneurs to have access to a wide consumer base and thereby allows entrepreneurs to enjoy the benefits of economies of scale. Identically, the role of per capita has been strangely observed to exert positive impact on the rate of rise in female entrepreneurs with workers.

Reasons for the Gap between Ideal & Actual Position of Women Entrepreneurs in India

Though Constitution has provided Indian women enough rights and protection to grow and develop in the cultural and economic space, still there lays a substantial gap between ideal and actual position. According to few commentators, (Tripathy, 2012) & (Ansari, 2016) the problems and constraints experienced by women entrepreneurs resulted in restricting the expansion of women entrepreneurship. The greatest deterrent in their pace of progress is their 'gender'. This patriarchal society itself plays the role of stumbling block. Male members always assume it as a big risk while financing the ventures run by women. Women are mostly being previewed as weaker sex. This orthodox perception itself acts as a barrier to entry for the woman entrepreneurs into business. Besides, women entrepreneurs always face stiff competition against their male counterpart who get easy access in the promotion and development area and can carry out easy marketing of their products with both the organized sector and rest of the male colleagues of the sector. Such a competition ultimately results in the liquidation of women entrepreneurs. Lack of enough self-confidence, will-power, outlook and optimistic attitude amongst women creates a fear psychosis. Moreover, their family members and the society are reluctant to stand beside their entrepreneurial growth. Besides, women in India lead a protected life. They are even less educated, economically not stable nor self-dependent, which reduce their ability to bear the risk and uncertainties involved in a business. In India women mobility is highly limited due to several reasons. A single women asking for room is still looked with suspicion. Cumbersome exercise involved in starting with an enterprise coupled with officials humiliating attitude towards women compels them to give up their spirit of surviving in enterprise altogether. Family obligation of rearing and bringing up the children also plays as major bar in their way of success in both developed and developing nations. The financial institutions discourage women entrepreneurs on the belief that they can at any time leave their business and become busy with their housed chores again. Indian women always give greater emphasis to family life and relationships. Therefore their business success solely depends on the support the family members extended to them in the business process and management.

However, as per Census of 2011, 48% population of India are females and gender equity has been declared to be achieved as top priority basis. The 12th five year plans has been identified the key elements of gender equity be addressed in the next five years as economic empowerment, physical and social infrastructure, enabling legislations, women's participation in governance, inclusiveness of all categories of vulnerable women, engendering national policies and mainstreaming gender through gender budgeting.

Domestic burden and legal constraint of family laws confine the women within her domestic drudgery and obstruct them from being successful entrepreneurs. Mahajan (2013) asserted that both institutional and legal environment is critical to the growth of female enterprises. In our patriarchal society, laws which govern the private domestic spheres are inherently tilted towards patriarchal rights. Therefore laws related to marriage, inheritance or land-ownership was all against rights of women since inception. The consequential amendments and changes, whichever came could not change the gross vision of the society at large scale and therefore problems persisted at the level of implementation. This hinders women's access to capital, which could otherwise be utilised as collateral for securing loans or start up capital for venturing new business.

Way Ahead

There has been a paradigm shift of demographics in Indian corporate landscape in recent years. The numbers of women penetrating in the business world keeping shoulder to shoulder to their male counterpart has been rising. The sheer confidence exuded by them brings about a fresh wind of change. The myth of 'glass ceiling for a woman' has to be completely busted with new entrepreneurial strides. Women should be institutionally mentored to be more confident and enterprising. They should be made aware about their latent potentials. Essential ingredients of enterprising women have been found to be 'clarity of thought', 'confidence of taking initiative', 'risk taking attitude'. Government should groom the aspirant women both in rural and urban sector to implant these virtues in them. Infrastructure is also very crucial for starting any new venture and therefore Government should set some priorities for women entrepreneurs for allocation of industrial plots, sheds and amenities. It has also been observed that Self Help Groups of women entrepreneurs have the ability to mobilize resources and pool capital funds in the field of industry, trade and commerce. Initiatives should be taken to raise the number of SHGs. However, unless and until the patriarchal perceptions on women participation in workforce is corrected, mere constitutional rights and gendered policy could hardly make any sea change.

References

Ansari, D.A., (2016). Women Entrepreneurship in India (An Empirical Study). *AEIJST*, 1-14.

Barbieri, P. (1999). Caratteristicheedevoluzione del lavoro-indipendentefemminile neglianniNovanta in Italia. In S. Negrelli, *Istituzioni e imprenditorialità femminile.* Guerini e Associat.

Butler, J. (1993). *Bodies that Matter.* New York: Routledge.

Connell, R. (1995). *Masculinities.* London: University of California Press.

Daymard, A. (2015). *Determinants of Female Entrepreneurship in India, OECD Economics Department Working Papers, No. 1191 http://dx.doi.org/10.1787/5js4rfh5gtbq-en.* Paris: OECD Publishing.

Gergen, K. (1982). *Toward Transformation in Social Knowledge.* New York: Springer-Verlag.

Gherardi, S. (2003). Feminist Theory and Organization Theory: A Dialogue on New Bases. In C. Knudsen, & H. Tsoukas, *Organizational Theory as Science:Prospects and Limitations.* Oxford: Oxford University Press.

Gherardi, S. (1995). *Gender, Symbolism and Organizational Cultures.* London: Sage.

Gherardi, S. (1994). The Gender We Think, The Gender We Do in Our Everyday Organizational Lives. *Human Relations*, 591-610.

Giddens, A. (1979). *Central Problems in Social Theory: Action, Structure and Contradictionin Social Analysis.* London: Macmillan.

Gherardi, S. ,B. Poggio. (2003). *Donna per fortuna, uomo per destino.* Milan: Etas.

Kobeissi, N. (2010). Gender factors and female entrepreneurship: International evidence and policy implications. *Journal of International Entrepreneurship*, 1-35.

Kolstad, I., A. Wiig. (2013). Is It Both What You Know And Who You Know? Human Capital, Social Capital and Entrepreneurial Success. *Journal of International Development*, 626-639.

Martin, P. (1993). Feminism and Management. In E. Fagenson, *Women inManagement: Trends, Perspective and Challenges.* Newbury Park, CA: Sage.

Minniti, M. ,W.Naudé. (2010). What Do We Know about the Patterns and Determinants of Female Entrepreneurship across Countries? *European Journal of Development Research*, 277-293.

Parker, S.C.,C.M. van Praag. (2006). (2006) "Schooling, Capital Constraints, and Entrepreneurial Performance: The Endogenous Triangle . *Journal of Business and Economic Statistics*, 416-431.

Sluis, Van der, J., M.Van Praag and W. Vijverberg. (2005). Entrepreneurship Selection and Performance: A Meta-Analysis of the Impact of Education in Developing Economies. *World Bank Economic Review*, 225-261.

Tripathy, A. L. (2012, November 16). *Women Entrepreneurs in India - Over the years!* Retrieved June 16, 2018, from FORE School of Management: Lal, Anita, Women Entrepreneurs in India - Over the Years! (November 15, 2012).http://dx.doi.org/10.2139/ssrn.2176377

West, C. D. Zimmerman. (1987). Doing Gender. *Gender and Society*, 125-151.

Zanfrini, L. (1999). *Immigrati, mercatidellavoro e programmazionedeiflussid'ingresso.* Milan: FondazioneCariplo.

Chapter - IV

A Study on Human Rights Violations in Nigeria-Biafra War: Patterns and Evolution

James Okolie-Osemene

Introduction

The Nigeria-Biafra war was fought mainly to sustain the existence of Nigerian state and prevent division of the country. The war was seen by the Igbo leaders as the only means of actualising the freedom of the Easterners from perceived marginalisation. This chapter was informed by the scenarios created during the war that it is difficult to crush a rebellion in a war situation without violating human rights. Kieh avers that Civil War consists of the following elements: issue area of disagreement between or among the parties; actors, the warring factions involved in the conflict; ideological beliefs that are pursued by parties; conflict context, which refers to the environment, conflict cycle, modes of war prosecution such as recruitment of combatants, military hardware and operational oversight. (Kieh, 2002) Any attempt to link the decision of the Eastern region to secede from Nigeria with the discovery of oil is not logical considering the fact that self determination can be hinged on survival rather than economic gains. For instance, the argument by Mohammed that

"Ojukwu and many Igbo intellectuals were inclined to secede at all cost; that Ojukwu would not have wanted to secede if there was no oil in East," (Mohammed, 1988) is too simplistic and has little or nothing to do with the proclamation of independence. It disregards the pogrom and hostilities against Igbo speaking people in most parts of the country prior to the war.

Protecting human rights during wars or armed conflicts has remained a challenge to various nations and international organisations. Human rights are standards that all societies are expected to uphold and this explains why the principles of human rights are equality, non-discrimination, indivisibility, inalienability, interdependency, universality, responsibility, and human dignity. Failure of actors to prioritise the inalienable, universal and indivisibility nature of human rights motivates abuses against vulnerable groups. The fact that human rights remain critical to sustainable livelihoods cannot be downplayed especially in war settings when laws of war are usually disregarded. Human rights remain highly critical in the life of every modern state in the international political system, and this makes the safety of all citizens an obligation for policy makers and law enforcement agencies. In spite the fact that the regulatory framework of protecting the rights of everybody is enshrined in the constitutions of nations and indeed various international instruments or protocols ratified by many states, the menace of human rights violations remains unabated.

While writing on how war is evil and the goodness associated with peace, Adanue revealed that most nations in the world adopted Mao Tse Tung's popular maxim that states 'make war to have peace' to heart in all its totality, with the assertion that war is a necessary condition for peace. The author questions this position from various destructions caused by war, particularly the Operation Desert Storm which ravaged Kuwait and Iraq in the early 1990s. The elusive nature of peace in Iraq and neighbouring countries today also point to the dangers of prosecuting war for peace as most of the countries in the Middle East have remained crisis ridden since the end of different wars during and towards the end of the Cold War. General Gowon cited the need to keep Nigeria one as the main goal of declaring war on Biafra which declared independence in May 1967. Both sides were exposed to one of the deadliest and longest wars in human history fought for more than two years.

Writing on the victims of war, Patricia Prestwich emphasises on the problem of mental exhaustion which is often associated with the victims of war. The author further elucidates the psychiatric theory which minimizes the psychological impact of war. (Prestwich, 2003) It is noteworthy that the trauma in armed conflicts is witnessed by belligerents and vulnerable groups around conflict prone areas which are battle zones or ambush/escape routes. Any study on human rights contributes to the knowledge of society because human rights protection concerns people in every society. The attention the issue of human right discourse has attracted would have been enough to addressing the problems arising from man's activities if it is given much needed priority. Existing literature suggests that any society that desires stability must recognize the rights of people both minorities and majority groups.

Modern human rights developed from the need to protect the inherent dignity and inalienable rights of all members of the human family from oppression and the need to set minimum standards for a civilised existence. The issue of human rights is a global phenomenon because it is situated within the contemporary conception of peace. This is because everybody requires the protection of inalienable rights to live peacefully without threat to his or her survival. This global phenomenon explains the relevance of safety in basic human needs.

Security forces and other stakeholders have an obligation to ensure respect for national laws, and international humanitarian and human rights laws, especially in countries witnessing armed conflicts. (Muhammedally, 2015) It has been suggested that security forces need to prioritise, learn, and put into practice civilian protection by undertaking in-depth, pre-mission and in-mission planning and training to avoid harm, and proactively protecting civilians, provision of security to returnees, as well as protection both from crime and revenge attacks. (Muhammedally, 2014) The issue of Nigeria Biafra war has been studied by scholars of history, conflict studies, war studies and even sociology. But it is necessary to revisit the human rights abuses recorded during the war to the detriment of the Biafran side.

Conceptual and Theoretical Explanations

As a concept, human rights continue to attract the attention of scholars. The idea of human rights declares that every individual has legitimate claims upon his or her own society for certain freedoms and benefits. (Henkin, 1989) Ajomo and Okagbue posit that human rights are those rights which all human beings enjoy by simple virtue of their humanity, the deprivation of which would constitute a grave affront to one's natural sense of justice. (Ajomo, Okagbue, 1991)

The theory that explains some factors that exacerbate human rights violation is hostility perception. Catildi posits that hostility perception theory states that the perception of the other is hostile toward one's own group or culture which tends to exacerbate conflict and conflict behaviour. Such conflict behaviour creates room for human rights abuses. (Cataldi, 2011) It should be noted that conflict-related violations are more dangerous than the socio-cultural violations and others. The relevance of this theory to the study is that during the period, the prosecution of the war was characterised by hostility perception and dehumanisation to the extent that human dignity was downplayed. The right to life which demanded that people should be treated with dignity was abused to the extent that civilians were even treated like combatants. In their numerous writing, various scholars identified the misuse of firearms during the war which they simply refer to as massacre or genocide. The litany of killings that dotted various villages became a source of fear. The sufferings that most Igbo indigenes were subjected to after the war would have been averted if the third party intervention adopted in pre-war years had worked. But the communication breakdown between leaders of Biafra and those of Nigeria in Lagos made the impasse a complex one.

The Challenges of Human Rights Protection During the War

The hostility that dotted relationship between the Igbos and other parts of Nigeria before, during and after the war can best be explained with the hostility perception theory which offers insight into how different ethnic groups manage their differences. The actions of the groups remain critical to peace or conflict. The problematic is that hostility perception has not only scathed intergroup relations efforts in Nigeria, but also remains one of the most malignant attributes of intergroup relations in the country's history. (Nwobueze, Okolie-Osemene, 2017) Hostility perception rather exposes the weakness of most groups in Nigeria in the management of social relations.

The arduous task of protecting and implementing human rights instruments cannot be downplayed given the complexities involved. There are apparent challenges that influence or hinder the protection of human rights in different contexts. Such challenges range from institutional accountability, to monitoring, environmental and national stability, philosophical explanations and contextualisation of the concept of right, the limit of recognition and implementation, policymakers' oversight, the inability of society to provide basic human needs, the politics of economic/ military sanctions and countersanctions, the perennial problem of gender inequality, regime types, state isolation as well as evolution of criminal states among others. In the context of Biafra, an issue that cannot be neglected is the use of economic blockade. Most of the aforementioned challenges greatly violate the concept of respect of human life which argues that people must avoid doing to others what is not good. In the case of Nigeria, it was a matter of sovereignty, with the aim of keeping the country united as one single entity. (Obasola, 2014) Various atrocities committed by officers as well as soldiers in the warfront were caused by their determination and directive to win the war at all cost and bring the Biafrans down to their knees in surrender. But it should be noted that the achievement of this war goal lasted longer than expected as the Biafran side which had little weapons to fight struggled to make the war last as they adopted different strategies to outrun the invasive plans of federal troops from many fronts. The frustration that set increased the violation of human rights in different occasions.

It was difficult to guarantee human security because two unequal belligerent parties were already enmeshed in a full blown war of survival. The violations that occurred in bushes and those that occurred in residential areas varied but had a lot of similarities. It is noteworthy that while some troops went as far as hiding in bushes using grasses and fresh leaves of plants, unsuspecting combatants who posed threat to some of the belligerents were fired with weapons. To a great extent, some federal troops may have justified their activities in residential areas when they broke into homes and shot at civilians with the excuse that they combed communities to get rid of the enemy forces, but such acts contravened the laws of war.

It should be noted that different scholars have tried to examine the war within the context of the just war theory which explains the justifications for the decision to wage war on opponents. However, the aim of this article is not to theorise the rightfulness or wrongness of the war or whether Nigeria gave adequate opportunity for peaceful management of the conflict without adopting a confrontational strategy, but to reveal the nature of human rights abuses during the war.

While both sides attempted to justify the war, they have been blamed for failing to allow third party intervention succeeds. While Nigeria justified the police action that escalated hostilities on the need to protect territorial integrity of the country, Biafra also justified the secession on her right to self determination and to prevent the annihilation of the Igbos even without much weapons and adequate food for survival. This eventually frustrated Biafra's war goals.

On the Igbo's option of secession for the actualisation of a sovereign state, China Achebe argues that:

> The Nigerian military Government cannot claim to be genuinely interested in the progress and welfare of the Nigerian people while at the same time inflicting the bloodiest warfare on the people of Nigeria and employing unscrupulous foreign mercenaries in a total war that really destroys hundreds of people and the economy of our nation... The people of Biafra have a right to fight a Government that has constantly treated its people to the most savage forms of brutality and persists in denying these people its fundamental human rights while claiming to represent other interests. (Achebe, 2012)

The government did little to curb the abuse of laws of war by the troops, rather focused on strengthening military and grand strategy for victory. While crushing the rebellion remained the priority of government, interest was not shown to regulate the operational oversight of commanders that pushed to defeat the seceding new state.

The foregoing made Adanue to argue that:

> Throughout history, war or violence has always been advocated as the quickest and the surest means for righting wrong, because as it is claimed, the oppressor, for instance, will never peacefully and voluntarily give freedom to the oppressed, since it is part of the oppressors' plan to keep the oppressed in a perpetual state of domination.

The domination was repeatedly cited by the leaders of defunct Biafra and many Igbos who lost their sources of livelihood the manifestation of what Owalabi described as the perception of the "other" or ethnocentrism. (Owolabi, 2003) Achebe noted that Obafemi Awolowo's ambition for power and the advancement of Yoruba interest made him to see Igbos as being too domineering to the extent that he welcomed the policy of starvation effected through economic blockade. (Achebe, 2012) This eventually led to death of young Igbos.

The war which was highly publicised by international media such as the New York Times, Reuters, Associated Press among others, escalated despite the mediatory efforts of then Pope Paul VI and did not receive desired intervention by the United Nations which had more words than action in view of containing the war by calling the belligerent parties to order. According to Aneke thousands of the American Committee to keep Biafra Alive demonstrated at the United Nations (UN) headquarters in New York on 8 August, 1968 to demand for a UN intervention in the plight of the starving Biafrans. (Aneke, 2007) Their right to food was violated by Nigeria's war policies which not only frustrated various relief efforts by many international humanitarian groups by insisting that aid/relief groups would not be allowed to supply foods directly to Biafran territory. This policy manifested in economic blockade that targeted Biafra. The foregoing issue on starvation of the Easterners was captured by then head of the Biafran Republic, General Odumegwu Ojukwu in his 'cry to the world':

> ...for three years we have fought against overwhelming odds...We had relied on the conscience of the world to respect the rights of our people to self determination and security. We have been frustrated by an international conspiracy against the interest of the African...Nigeria's insistence to control the distribution of relief is both to ensure that Biafrans get no such relief and also to shut out outsiders who might witness and expose the enormous crimes she plans to commit against our people. Nigeria

> throughout this war has distinguished herself for a lack of control over her armed forces. (Aneke, 2007)

The lamentation rather came too late as the consequences of declaring the secession which motivated the war should have been given proper consideration before announcing independence of Biafra. The fact that Chukwuemeka Odumegwu Ojukwu made the statement after leaving Biafra for his second in command Philip Effiong to negotiate peaceful surrender revealed that the defunct new was never prepared to exist from the first day when the idea was conceived. The fact that the Nigerian government failed to control her troops in an attempt to invade and capture secessionist territory explains why the period 1967-1970 was characterised by the violation of human rights. The abuse of human dignity made life more brutish than ever in the history of Igbo people whose tradition abhors the killing of fellow human beings.

The duty of a commander in chief who declared war and even threatened the downfall of the enemy troops is to ensure the safety of his citizens and prevent them from suffering some humanitarian crisis within his capacity. These abuses were caused by Commanders' bid to handle enemies as rebels. Although treating rival parties as rebels enhances the psychological strength of troops, it downplays violates the laws of war.

The frustration of both sides motivated the starvation and killing of innocent civilians during the war. One of the reasons why human rights violations during the early years of the war from 1967 to the first quarter of 1968 was that the level of frustration was still low so much so that the belligerent parties still expected victory within a short time. But this conviction was short-lived as the war neither ended nor showed any signs of possible truce as the actors increased their weaponry through multiple sources owing to their access to the security market. Consequently, they were more armed with the weapons of human rights abuses and determination to eliminate their rival combatants. Sadly, the determination was taken to civilians who became the targets of vengeance.

The costs of not going to war or declaration of the sovereign state of Biafra would have been lesser than the consequences of the war. For instance, Aneke stated that "a decree issued in Lagos on 15 January 1970 targeted those government workers who supported the Biafran movement or engaged hostile acts against the federal or state governments between Jan 15, 1966 and Jan 15, 1970. Gen. Gowon signed the decree which authorised disciplinary action against officers whose records revealed that they showed undue enthusiasm beyond the scope of their calling as civil servants in furthering the rebellion." (Aneke, 2007) As a result of the role they played during the war in which Mid-West fell to Biafra, Edo people called on the Federal Military Government to embark on tougher measures and not to recruit Igbos in Mid West for allegedly treacherously working against the federal troops. (Don't recruit Mid-West Ibos, 1967) These people forgot that enlistment into the army in time of war is an easy road to death and that no reasonable man would join the army in wartime.

As seen from Benhamin Adekunle's exposition on his role in the war that killed many, most Nigerian troops were accused of night lootings and robberies in most parts of Igboland especially during and after successful liberation of towns and villages governed by Biafra. The problem of this criminal behaviour of the Nigerian soldiers exposed the vulnerable groups to more danger to the extent that they had to grapple with both the trauma of war and banditry at the same time.

Heerten and Moses notes that "throughout the conflict, federal aircraft shelled towns and other targets on Biafran territory, frequently inflicting numerous civilian casualties." (Heerten, Moses, 2014) In their "mission to kill", Nigerian pilots switched off the engines of planes before flying low to bomb civilians, and this made Biafran Government to issue public safety warning on safe colours of clothes. (Achebe, 2012) The bombing of civilian populated areas and markets aggravated the crisis of food insecurity and associated starvation. This challenge according to Achebe "created a difficult proposition in finding food and made women to wake up very early in the morning from 4:00am to attend the daily markets to procure food; and when the Nigerians found out where the open markets were and started bombing them, the women moved their commercial activities to dense forests." (Achebe, 2012) The action of Nigerian air force showed their poor value for human life and this exposed people to danger, with their freedom of movement denied. The incessant bombing of markets violated the right to life and the laws of war. However, the relocation of open markets from the towns to forests demonstrated the doggedness of women who became breadwinners in some homes that lost their men in the war. It also showed the relevance of forests reserves to human security as they became safe havens to many. The period of the war was different from contemporary scenario where some forests are hideouts for insurgents, kidnappers or ritualists.

Despite General Gowon's operational code of conduct in war situation, commanders did not prevent the Asaba massacre which occurred after many Igbos residing in Benin and Sapele had faced victimisation; and from 5 October 1967 life was no longer the same for the people of Asaba where some people narrowly escaped death when dead bodies prevented bullets from hitting them. (Bird, Ottanelli, 2014) As perceived relatives of Easterners, the people were regarded as sympathizers of the rebels who deserved no mercy. (Heerten, Moses, 2014) The massacre in Asaba was the height of human rights violations.

The fact that majority of Asaba people lost their family members and places of abode to the war even after spending weeks and months in the bushes as the case may be showed the magnitude of human rights abuses perpetrated by Nigerian soldiers. This caused a burden on women who had to rebuild their families after the loss of their husbands to the firepower of the federal troops. The abominable acts of the troops violated the traditional practices of the indigenous people whose rights to befitting burial rites were flagrantly abused while the town became synonymous with blood. The killings during the war created scenarios of targets, victims, offenders and aggressive behaviour in the history of warfare.

The use of rape as a punishment on the men around present day Anioma violated women's right to human dignity. According to Bird and Ottanelli "rape was a challenge to men's rights over 'their' women" mainly because it brought emotional trauma on both the victims and their husbands who watched the act on their own wives as troops climbed on them. (Bird, Ottanelli, 2014) Beautiful women were also forced to marry some officers with sudden disappearance from the sight of their family members. Both rape and massacre were the sources of family disintegration during the Nigeria-Biafra war as many families lost their parents and siblings.

The sacrilegious acts of the belligerent parties were beyond the Asaba massacre in which deaths occurred from house to house before the Ogbe-Osowa massacre the next day. In some villages around Ika, some soldiers forcefully took people's wives and threatened to kill their husbands. Even young women began dating the soldiers with impunity according to key informants at Ekuku Agbor in Ika South Local Government Area. This strange act made well behaved young women to stop appearing in public for the period when the troops camped in the villages while those that needed to go out for different reasons had to dress like old women to prevent the troops from sexually harassing them. Oral sources also reveal that when Nigerian soldiers blocked the highways, they stopped commuters, ordered them out of vehicles and even buried some of them alive. This created panic in various villages.

The spatial nature of the human rights abuses during the war shows that Igbo speaking parts of Biafra recorded higher violations with the loss of property and lives than non-Igbo speaking communities in present day Cross River State and Rivers State. Out of all the human rights abuses, three were highly reprehensible: the burying of people alive, the rape of women and girls, and group massacre that occurred in Asaba. All these abuses did not receive much intervention of the international community as far as the crime against humanity is concerned.

Although both belligerent parties had limitations as far as military power was concerned due to a lack of funds, personnel, discipline and education, Nigeria's strategic advantage over Biafra was the diplomatic status of the country globally as it already had international statehood recognition. (Heerten, Moses, 2014) It was easier for Nigeria which was already a member of the United Nations, the Commonwealth of Nations and the Organisation of African Unity to embark on diplomatic discussions with other states to frustrate the Biafra agenda. No doubt, fighting such an intra-state armed conflict with diplomatic advantage gave Nigeria a strategic boost beyond the battlefield. This eventually discouraged many sovereign states from recognising Biafra as the Federal Government already had direct access to the security market thereby leaving the Biafrans with the option of patronising the black market for weaponry. At a period when the blockade affected Biafra's grand strategy, the country had to look inward to utilise available human and material resources. However, despite the innovative efforts of the Biafran Research and Production unit in manufacturing Ogbunigwe bombs, the Biafran soldiers and civilians were not shielded from the bout of human rights violations during the war.

As seen from the story of Nigeria, Nigerian soldiers were involved in indiscriminate killing of unarmed civilians to the extent that the gory pictures of children affected by kwashiorkor in Biafra was crime against humanity. The fact that the Biafran offensives were facilitated by mercenaries from South Africa, The Congo, Belgium and Yemen, who were already knowledgeable about grand strategy, did not prevent high casualties on the part of Biafra. Human rights were violated through the establishment of various operations by the Nigerian troops to push inwards Biafran towns. While Major Williams from South Africa said his interest in fighting on the side of Biafra was a choice, Marc Goossens from Belgium described Biafran soldiers as very brave but it should be noted that brevity does little to prevent human rights violations in war situations especially when the enemy has superior fire power. He noted that Nigerian side had more weapons with heavy tanks more than Biafra. (Olanrewaju, 2007) The use of foreign mercenaries in defence of Biafra exposed the dilemma of a newly formed state, and weakness of Biafra's military and grand strategy with armed forces that required adequate training. The mixed role played by the Great Powers is noteworthy. It is noteworthy that Britain, Russia, USA and France did little to end the war as some of them sold arms to both sides and still went ahead to provide humanitarian relief to the war torn Biafra. This double standard role escalated the armed conflict.

Wole Soyinka warned that there would be no victory for anyone in the war, but only a repetition of human and material wastage and a superficial control that must one day blow up in the faces of the citizens. (Aneke, 2007) The inhuman experiences of Anioma people (Oshimili, Aniocha and Ika) made most of them to rebuke anyone suggesting or clamouring for a sovereign state of Biafra any time still feel caught in the middle. The trauma of war which they suffered in the hands of federal soldiers is responsible for their lack of interest in supporting any agitation that may attract militarism or even initiatives to associate them with Biafra Memorial Day as usually marked in Southeast. (Bird, Ottanelli, 2014) The incident in Asaba made many elders around this location to mock at the youth who only heard from the media and oral sources but never witnessed the war. Sadly, Biafra war memorial has always been marked by lethal violence due to clashes between security forces and the unarmed-peaceful protesters.

Conclusion

This study has shown that war is destructive to humanity. The increase in human rights violations during the war was caused by the determination of belligerent parties to conquer one another in order to emerge victorious and nip differences in the bud once and for all. This is one of the attributes of every conflict but the problem is that their ambitions undermined the rights of civilians who knew little or nothing about the sources of the war that made some of them to lose their family members and sources of livelihood. The role of ethnocentrism in aggravating hostility perception before and during the war cannot be downplayed. It is remarkable that the importation of weapons from different security markets, including those of Soviet Union and Britain escalated the war with attendant refugee crisis. The outcome of the war which manifested in human rights abuses and eventual surrender by Biafra was occasioned by the superiority of Nigerian in military strategy, weaponry, and even combatants to the extent that they had better training than the Biafran troops.

The dramatic nature of the war manifested in the manner in which most people from all walks of life such as poets, scholars, security personnel, artisans, students, traders and many others welcomed the idea of handling firearms to defend their new state. While some fought for a short time and withdrew or disappeared for safety, others fought till the end. However, those that became fallen heroes were not lucky as they died through the firepower of the Nigerian soldiers. Even some of the ex-combatants who survived the war suffered one deformity or the other like a neighbour whose deplorable partial deafness was caused by the war. He volunteered to fight for Biafra from Ubulu-Uku in present day Delta State. This chapter argues that both sides abused human rights but that of the Nigerian side was aggravated by the desperation to conquer breakaway towns and keep the country united. Given that war is usually a hostile form of intergroup relations, it would have been better if Biafra sought for the diplomatic support of various countries in Africa and wider world before declaring a sovereign state rather than establishing a new state without adequate provision for human and material resources needed to sustain it. The option of referendum would have been life-saving approach than the hasty state declaration. By implication, funds and time would not have been expended on humanitarian relief materials and charitable activities. The paper recommends that socio-economic justice, tolerance and informal peace education can become effective antidotes to secessionist agitation.

References

Achebe, C., (2012). *There was a Country: A personal history of Biafra.* New York: Penguin Books Ltd.

Ajomo, A.M., I.E. Okagbue. (1991). *Human Rights and the Administration of Criminal Justice in Nigeria.* Lagos: Nigerian Institute of Advanced Legal Studies.

Aneke, L.N. (2007). *The untold story of the Nigeria-Biafra war: A chronological reconstruction of the events and circumstances of the Nigerian Civil War.* New York: Triumph Publishing.

Bird, Elizabeth S., Fraser Ottanelli. (2014). er. The Asaba massacre and the Nigerian civil war: reclaiming hidden history . *Journal of Genocide Research*, 379-399.

Cataldi, R. (2011). Clash of Perceptions: Hostility Perception and the US-Muslim World Relationship. *Journal of Peace, Conflict & Development*, 27-46.

Don't recruit Mid-West Ibos. (1967, September 2). *Daily Times*, p. 8.

Heerten, Lasse A. Dirk Moses. (2014). The Nigeria–Biafra war: postcolonial conflict and the question of genocide. *Journal of Genocide Research,* 169-203.

Henkin, L. (1989). The Universality of the Concept of human rights. *The Annals of the American Academy of Political and Social Science*, 10-16.

Kieh, G. K. (2002). Civil Wars in Africa: Now and then. In E. E. Osaghae, E. Onwudiwe, & R. Suberu, *The Nigerian Civil War and its Aftermath: Civil Wars in Africa: Now and then* (pp. 8-25). Ibadan, Nigeria: John Archers Publishers.

Mohammed, A. R. (1988). The Nigerian Civil War 1967-1970 – A critical look at the developments that led to it. In U. Eleazu, *Nigeria: The first 25 years* (pp. 73-77). Ibadan: Heinemann Educational Books Ltd.

Muhammedally, S. (2014, July 16). *Don't Forget the Civilians in the Fights against ISIS.* . Retrieved June 17, 2018, from The Atlantic Council: http://www.atlanticcouncil.org/blogs/menasource/don-t-forget-the-civilians-in-the-fight-against-isis

Muhammedally, S. (2015). Iraq: "Learning Civilian Protection the Hard Way." . *Stability: International Journal of Security & Development*, 1-7.

Nwobueze, C. C., J. Okolie-Osemene. (2017). Hostility perception: Theoretical analysis of intergroup relation in Nigeria. *International Journal of Peace and Conflict Studies (IJPCS)*, 1-8.

Obasola, K. (2014). Ethical perspective of human life in relation to human rights in African indigenous societies. *International Review of Social Sciences and Humanities*, 29-35.

Olanrewaju, J. (2007). *Naij: A History of Nigeria.* Actualize Production.

Owolabi, O. (2003). Fictional Tribes and Tribal Fictions: Ethnicity, Ethnocentrism and the Problem of the "Other" in Africa,PEFS Monograph New Series No.4. Ibadan: John Archers Publishers Ltd.

Prestwich, E.,P. (2003). "Victims of War"? Mentally-Traumatized Soldiers and the State, 1918-1939. In *Proceedings of the Western Society for French History Vol. 31* (pp. 243-254).

Chapter - V

Violation of Human Right: Trafficking of Women — An Understanding

— *Susmita Bhattacharyya*

Introduction

All persons, regardless of gender, are entitled to enjoy all basic human rights; sometimes women are often denied these rights simply because they are women. In the context of trafficking, many basic rights of women are violated e.g. the right to be free from all forms of discrimination. Due to the unequal nature of gender relations, women and girl-children constitute the majority of those who are trafficked. 'Women's rights are human rights' – so this is not claiming 'special rights' for women. It must be recognized that women have the same basic human rights as men. Many women are deprived of their rights because some societies consider women inferior to men. There the mainstream population denies their access to justice, participation in political life and the ability to make personal life decisions.

Trafficking in human beings is one of the most serious human rights violations prevalent today. Human trafficking is a lucrative business, internationally. It involves transfer of persons by fraudulent means. (Watson, Silkstone, 2006)

According to International Organization for Migration (IOM), in 2011 IOM has supported individual trafficked persons on 5,498 occasions. Out of them, 62 per cent of them were women. 53 per cent of them were trafficked mainly due to forced labour and 27 per cent were sexually exploited. Violations of human rights can be viewed both as a cause and a consequence of trafficking in human beings. Trafficking is a cause of human rights violations, as the act of trafficking violates human rights. The human rights of trafficked persons who are treated as commodities rather than human beings are violated because they are exploited to some extent, are deprived of their freedom of movement, often denied access to health care and, in the worst case scenario, deprived of their right to life. Trafficking is also a consequence of human rights violations, as trafficked persons, particularly women, have frequently experienced rights violations prior to being trafficked, exposing them more to the risk of exploitation and abuse. Trafficking as a social incidence deserves attention for last few decades in India. It is mostly seen that women and girl children are the worst victims in this context. Human trafficking is perceived as a situation where one or more person holds possession of another person for compelled service (Misra, 2013). Veerendra Misra pointed out that process, means and purpose should be considered as significant in the sphere of trafficking.

The definition of trafficking in human beings of the Protocol to Prevent, Suppress and Punish Trafficking in Persons, especially Women and Children, which was signed in Palermo in 2000 and came into force in December 2003 (commonly known as the Palermo Protocol). Article 3a of the Palermo Protocol defines trafficking in human beings as: The recruitment, transportation, transfer, harbouring or receipt of persons, by means of the threat or use of force or other forms of coercion, of abduction, of fraud, of deception, of the abuse of power or of a position of vulnerability or of the giving or receiving of payments or benefits to achieve the consent of a person having control over another person, for the purpose of exploitation. Exploitation shall include, at a minimum, the exploitation of the prostitution of others or other forms of sexual exploitation, forced labour or services, slavery or practices similar to slavery, servitude or the removal of organs.

The definition of trafficking in human beings contains three elements,

1. **The activity:** the recruitment, transport, transfer, harbouring or receipt of a person;
2. **The means:** threat or use of force or other forms of coercion, of abduction, of fraud, of deception, of the abuse of power or of a position of vulnerability or of the giving or receiving of payments or benefits to achieve the consent of a person having control over another person;
3. **The purpose:** the exploitation of the prostitution of others or other forms of sexual exploitation, forced labour or services, slavery or practices similar to slavery, servitude or the removal of organs.

OBJECTIVES: In this article the researcher has some objectives. These are –

(1) to clarify the response pattern of trafficking of women,
(2) to determine the causes,
(3) to describe the effects and
(4) to discuss the recommendations for prevention of trafficking of women.

Trafficked women are linked with certain features of deprivation in general. Trafficked women are usually poor and less educated. Some of them are not even literate. They can even be homeless. Usually, they are socially vulnerable. According to International Organization for Migration, traffickers capitalize on deprivations created by endless civil disturbances, war, unemployment etc. Commodification of women's bodies augments the deprivation of the social, political and economic power of the trafficked women. These are – deprivation of the right to equality, safety, dignity and equality. A trafficked girl can be related with several problems in her life. She is displaced from her community. She can be procured illegally and sold and brought by somebody. She can be wrongly confined and physically tortured. She can be mentally exploited also. A clear supply chain can be located in this connection. 'The chain may be long or short depending on the number of persons and the places involved' (Nair, 2010). The probable places include village, recruitment spotter, village bus stop, alighting railway station, transit through railways, embarking railway station and so on. On the basis of analysis it is observed that there are some general indicators of trafficking of women. Exploitation is associated with this phenomenon. Sometimes more than one person is linked with this factor. Monetary transaction can act as added attraction behind this activity. 'The exploiter would have established adequate safety valves, protective measures and chain of command to ward off any onslaught by law enforcement agencies or other exploiters or media.

P.M. Nair also admitted that nexus of the exploiters with other exploiters and even responders is another generic indicator. This kind of nexus can be based on friendship also. There are also some specific indicators. Women are displaced from their original communities to the exploited communities. Transportation is a need in this phase. There can be plurality of transit points. Trafficked women are victims. Their vulnerability is linked with lack of awareness of rights, support system. Poor response systems create more problems here.

The response pattern involves following components.

— 3 P's	• PREVENTION • PROTECTION • PROSECUTION
— 5 R's	• RESCUE • RESTORATION • REPATRIATION • REHABILITATION • REINTEGRATION

Prevention as a mechanism includes required programmes and policies for empowering the 'vulnerable' persons, intervention in the transit areas, demand for proactive and punitive steps for punishment, all kinds of function for transformation of policies and legal matters. Thus an integrative and holistic prevention system can be developed. Protection implies all kinds of care as well as attention to the victim [sometimes rescued person]. As a consequence the person concerned can be turned into an empowered personality. Protection includes rehabilitation programmes also. According to Nair [2010], prosecution includes identification of the offenders, tracing them, taking action against them, bringing them to justice, getting them punished and initiating all post conviction activities. Rescue involves a step where a trafficked woman or a woman likely to be trafficked should be transferred to a safer place for protection of her right. Restoration involves a shift of place for the victim within the periphery of country. Repatriation is a process of restoration outside the country. Rehabilitation is a necessary step for proper living of the victims in general. Reintegration includes many steps for normal living of the victims. It incorporates the concepts like dignified livelihood, security, empowerment in a total understanding. There should be a focus of time factor. Response pattern of the system needs a considerable amount of time. The time is not uniformly fixed for all the victims. The factor is completely dependent on situation. Contemporary approach of response pattern is linked with counselling and detraumatization.

CAUSE: There are basically some prominent causes behind the incidence of trafficking of women. Socio-cultural practices play important role in this context. Patriarchal ideology is the sole responsible factors here. Trafficking of women is clearly related with incidences like marriage and prostitution. Sometimes economic issues become the dominating force behind trafficking of women. There the role of family deserves attention. On the basis of the study it is shown that certain families are directly or indirectly involved in the trafficking process. Their ignorance, lack of livelihood options arising out of poverty, prevailing cultural traditions, or commercial motives could be the reasons behind this. There are plenty of instances of family members getting lured by traffickers, falling prey to their evil designs and, thereupon, allowing their wards to be trafficked. (Nair, Sen, 2004) Unavailability of education produces lack of awareness among the common mass in general. Hence they can't be properly conscious about the phenomenon.

Social Determinants of Trafficking

The social position of women: patriarchal stereotypes and domestic violence: The risk of being trafficked is linked with the position of women in the family and society as a whole. Thus the socio - cultural contexts have an effect on the risk of trafficking. Patriarchal values portray women as being inferior to men. This ideology indicates the position of women in wider periphery. Sometimes dysfunctional family situations, domestic violence may also push women and girls to leave home and make them more vulnerable to traffickers.

The position of women in the labour market: On the basis of information it can be said that poverty is the principal cause behind the incidences of trafficking. The main reason for persons to leave home was to work abroad. Therefore, the position in the labour market and the availability of equal opportunities in the labour market can be linked to the risk of trafficking.

EFFECTS: Trafficking has health, social, legal and economic effects on the victims. The effects can be two –fold. One set of effects are linked with individuals. Trafficked persons are reportedly traumatized and depressed by their experiences. Suicidal thoughts are commonly reported among them. The mental and emotional state of the survivors may include malevolence, helplessness and withdrawal; disassociation; self-blame and identification with the aggressor; distraction; a foreshortened view of time; normalisation and shaping, whereby the victims convince themselves that their experiences had to happen instead of viewing them as traumatic. Some of the psychiatric disorders among survivors of trafficking are listed as posttraumatic stress disorder, depressive disorder, dissociative disorders, psychotic disorders and eating disorders. Girls are made to bear the responsibility of upholding the family honour through their sexual purity/chastity. If they are trafficked into CSE (commercial sexual exploitation), they face additional stress because of the prevalent morality. Besides being stigmatized as outcasts and facing moral and legal isolation. Some of these women have managed to turn these experiences into personal empowerment within their communities. Second set of effects are associated with society as a whole. The crime of trafficking is not only violation of a whole gamut of laws but also deprivation of human rights. Trafficking 'threatens the very fabric of society' because it involves not only criminals but also law enforcers. It manifests and perpetuates patriarchal attitudes and behaviour, which undermine the efforts to promote gender equality and eradicate discrimination against women and children. (Nair, Sen, 2004)

Recommendations

First and foremost necessity is a sense of urgency with humanistic orientation with passion. Laws should be engaged with effective and sustainable provisions for the protection of the victims. Insensitive attitude of the law enforcement agencies need to be addressed as soon as possible. They need to look at the issue, sensitively. The essentially masculine and androcentric values need to be done away from the State agencies. In many countries, inclusion of more women in law enforcement agencies tackling human trafficking, have improved the overall situation. Media must give sufficient priority on this issue. Proper coordination becomes very essential for combating the incidences. Local leaders should be involved in this context. Regional initiatives must be taken for the success of the activity. Better results are assured with the use of regional database for this matter. Similarly, sharing of good practice models and important judgments of the courts in the region could be considered for further implementation. Regional victim-witness protection protocols could be developed and circulated to all concerned for guidance. In this situation help lines and help booths are highly recommended mechanisms. Collaboration between governmental agencies and NGOs are truly helpful for execution of the programme. Public awareness campaigns must be arranged for solving the problem. Extensive and sustained awareness programmes can be effective in this arena. Sensitization approach must be taken for the success of the programmes in general. Role of family is very much crucial in the aspect for controlling the situations of trafficking of women in particular. Hence family must be considered as an important component in this activity.

It is well known fact that prevention of trafficking of women needs a holistic understanding within as well as outside community. Involvement and cooperation go hand in hand in this matter. The situation can't change by the legislative measure only. Several socio- cultural issues become very significant in the analysis of the scenario. Among the issues lack of livelihood opportunity, gender centric structure, deprivation of opportunity are worth mentioning. A different thought process should be developed with the focus of honour of humanity. Respect towards women must be taught as essential for every aspect. Emphasis must be put on value education to transform the entire socio –philosophical understanding of society in general. Trafficking of women initially was linked to the 'culture of silence'. Trafficking itself is an activity with a clandestine nature. People normally avoid such circumstances with their conscious escapism. (Pearson, 2000) Now entire gamut of society has transformed with 'community involvement Strategy' of NGO was described by E. Pearson in the following way —

Table 6.1: Community Involvement Strategy

	Local/National	*Regional*	*International*
a. Services b. Provision	– Set up shelter for victims of trafficking – Counselling – Information about migration – Family support – legal services – Comprehensive health care	– Assist trafficked persons during repatriation process – Welcome and initiate new migrants	– Support local NGOs in the process of repatriation and reintegration – Welcome and initiate new migrants
c. Research/ Documen-tation	– Document cases at immigrant detention centre – Mapping of villages in border areas – Research on working and living conditions of migrant workers especially in unregulated sector	– Research on migrants' repatriation and reintegration programmes between countries of origin/transit and destination	– Coordinate comparative analysis of impact of trafficking, immigration, labour and prostitution laws on trafficked persons
d. Informa-tion/ Education	– Meet with officials and share selected information about cases with them – Provide gender sensitivity or human rights training – Organize migration information campaign in villages in countries of origin	– Send information or documentation to regional mechanisms e.g. European, American or African Commissions – conduct regional human rights trainings for NGOs and relevant agencies	– Send information or documentation to international mechanisms e.g. Special Rapporteur on violence against women, Special Rapporteur on Human Rights of Migrants, Commission on Human Rights, CEDAW – coordinate international campaign to raise awareness about NGOs in countries of destination
e. Advocacy	– Public demonstration – Letter– writing to government – Lobby government on existing laws, policies and practices	– Lobby at regional conferences such as meetings of regional UN agencies, ASEAN, SAARC, EU, OAS, OAU – Campaigns/ action alerts	– Lobby relevant bodies of the UN and international bodies such as ILO, World Bank – Petition action

Source: E. Pearson, *Human Rights and Trafficking in Persons.*

Table 6.2: Activities at Different Levels

	Local/National	*Regional*	*International*
a. Services provision	- set up shelter for victims of trafficking - counselling - information about migration - family support - legal services - comprehensive health care	- assist trafficked persons during repatriation process - welcome and initiate new migrants	- support local NGOs in the process of repatriation and reintegration - welcome and initiate new migrants
b. Research/ Documentation	- document cases at immigrant detention centre - mapping of villages in border areas - research on working and living conditions of migrant workers especially in unregulated sector	- research on migrants' repatriation and reintegration programmes between countries of origin/transit and destination	- coordinate comparative analysis of impact of trafficking, immigration, labour and prostitution laws on trafficked persons

Source: E. Pearson, *Human Rights and Trafficking in Persons.*

According to a Report of the Secretary General of the United Nations, it is positive that the States are slowly adhering to the international instruments. The judiciary, police and prosecutors are being trained to address to the complex and high-impact crime of trafficking. National action plans and coordination bodies need to be effective to track the crime and boost resources to arrest trafficking. The knowledge base and awareness level regarding trafficking of women and girls need to be enhanced. Trafficking of women and girls need to be tackled from the human rights' perspective. Criminalization of all forms of trafficking of women and girls need to be developed according to standards put forward by the United Nations Convention against Transnational Organized Crime. Severe penalties should be included by the State laws. United Nations has through its 1949 Convention for the Suppression of the Traffic in Persons and of the Exploitation of the Prostitution of Others, 1979 Convention on the Elimination of All Forms of Discrimination against Women, 1989 Convention on the Rights of the Child and the 2000, the United Nations Convention against Transnational Organized Crime, its Protocol against the Smuggling of Migrants by Land, Sea and Air, and its Protocol to Prevent, Suppress and Punish Trafficking in Persons, especially Women and Children, the Human Rights Committee, the Committee on Economic, Social and Cultural Rights, the Committee on the Elimination of Racial Discrimination and the Committee against Torture etc all aim at uprooting the crime of trafficking of women and girls. The seriousness of the crime has been well understood by the international agencies. This will assist the policy makers and the executive to devise strategies to help the victims of trafficking. The links between the national and the international levels may be carefully identified and busted. Promoting dialogue and partnership would increase visibility regarding sharing of information and tracking the traffickers. (The United Nations Response to Trafficking in Women and Girls, 2002) NGOs should take initiatives for addressing the vulnerabilities. Their workable effort can transform the 'culture of silence' into 'zero tolerance'. (Nair, 2010) Human right counselling centres can be mostly helpful in this context. Media can use pamphlets and essential write ups with stories of trafficking. Thus people will be aware of the realistic situation of trafficking. Trafficking–free society can be achieved with a holistic effort from all round involvement. Exercise of human right can be possible with the complete absence of trafficking in all sphere of life. Trafficking of women is not only a matter of disgrace to society as a whole, but it also hampers empowerment of women in a negative way. Hence this kind of activity should be stopped with all possibilities for the sake of societal development at large.

References

Misra, V. (2013). *Human Trafficking –The Stakeholders' Perspective.* New Delhi: Sage.

Nair, P. (2010). *Human Trafficking, Konark Publishers Private Limited, 2010.* New Delhi: Konark Publishers Private Limited.

Nair, P.M., S. Sen. (2004). *A Report on Trafficking in Women and Children in India 2002-2003.* New Delhi: National Human Right Commission.

Pearson, E. (2000). *Human Rights and Trafficking in Persons.* Retrieved February 15, 2017, from Global Alliance against Traffic: http://www.gaatw.org

The United Nations Response to Trafficking in Women and Girls . (2002, November 8). Retrieved May 5, 2018, from Division for the Advancement of Women, United Nations: http://www.un.org/womenwatch/daw/egm/trafficking2002/reports/WP-DAW.PDF

Watson, Joy, Christine Silkstone. (2006). Human Trafficking as a Form of Gender-Based Violence: Protecting the Victim. *Agenda: Empowering Women for Gender Equity, No. 70, Gender-Based Violence Trilogy, Volume 1,2: Trafficking*, 110-118.

Chapter - VI

From Welfare to Rights: Growth of Children's Rights Movement in India

— ***Sutapa Ghosh***

Introduction

Development of the children is pre-condition of human development. (Covell, 2012) No society will be developed if it denies the access to development to children irrespective of caste, sex, religion and race. It is known fact that human development and human rights go hand in hand. Axford observes that there is a general consensus that some individual interests and liberties are so essential that all States and human beings should respect them. Designating those rights implies that they should take precedence over the private interests of those in power and the pursuit of other social goals and aspirations. Further, society needs to secure them, irrespective of traditions, history or levels of economic development. (Axford, 2008)

This belief is expressed in international law. 1948 United Nations Declaration of Human Rights mentions:

> "The adoption in 1948 by the United Nations of the Universal Declaration of Human Rights—the

> foundational document of the human rights movement... the Universal Declaration underscored its arrogance by proclaiming itself the "common standard of achievement for all peoples and nations." (Matua, 2011)

In a developing country like India, children should be the first priority in developmental activities. Children share 39 per cent of the total population in India. (Statistics of Children in India, 2017) The Government of India views children as a 'supremely important national asset' (Rao, 2007). If there was no child, there would be no humanity and there cannot be a universe without humanity. Moral sense of the society compels us to search for a solution to the problems of the children. In principle, every child has a right to love and be loved. The future wellbeing of a nation depends on how its children grow and develop.

Every society needs to devote total attention to ensure that children are properly cared for and brought up in a proper atmosphere. They should receive adequate training, education and guidance so that they may be able to have their rightful place in society when they grew up. (Wal, 2006)

Kosuri quoted Justice K. Subba Rao, the former Chief Justice of India who asserted,

"Social justice must begin with children. Unless a tender plant is properly tended and nourished, it has little chance of growing into a strong and useful tree. So, the first priority in the scale of social justice shall be given to the welfare of children." (Kosuri, 2013)

Early childhood is a vital and fragile period for the individual's growth. Developmental paucities during this stage lead to permanent hindrance in the physical and mental growth. Children are invisible because data gathered from any kind of survey never give significance to children. (John, 2003) The most surprising fact is that even in studies conducted on children, they themselves are ignored. Information is collected from the members of families, school teachers, activists, professional or bureaucrats. Therefore, their interests or problems are seen from the perspective of adult. Now-a-days a picture is emerging slowly revealing that children are one of the most neglected minorities of the world. Reality is that children can neither raise their voice nor they have the power to vote. Therefore, the adults have greater onus to plan for their development. In a recent survey conducted by Child Rights and You (CRY) (Bhattacharya, 2014) about the reflection of the children in the election agenda of many parties (including both the leftist and the rightist political parties) showed that in their respective manifestos only 11 percent space was provided to the various issues related to children. This indicated that none of them gave importance to children as they were perhaps invisible to them. The survey mentioned that the political parties have not felt the urgent necessity for bringing in overall development of children who constituted a major part of the citizens.

The United Nations adopted the Declaration of Children's Rights in 1924. The expanded version, the Declaration on the Rights of the Child was adopted in 1959. This declaration was based on a belief that all children should have the right to enjoy childhood, like a time to play, preserve their innocence and receive protection from the atrocities of the adult world. The weaknesses of these two declarations were that both of them ignored the cultural differences among the Members States of the United Nations and did not pay adequate attention to the views of the children. After 20 years, due to renewed interest on children rights, The United Nations Convention on the Rights of the Child (CRC) was adopted in 1989. This was adopted by the members of the UN except two. United States of America and Somalia did not sign the CRC.

India has ratified the CRC in 1992. India has taken many steps to improve the conditions of the children compared to the earlier times. In the pre-independence era, many social reformers took active part to educate the children and restrain child marriages. Since Independence, various initiatives have been undertaken as part of welfare activities. Many programmes have also been adopted in the different Five Years Plans to improve the situation and protect children from abuses and exploitation. Initiatives are also taken to eradicate child labour, and reduce the drop-out rate in schools. Mid Day Meal (MDM) is a landmark programme of Government of India, initiated in 1995. It targets towards preventing child malnutrition and to bring them in school. The aim of the programme is to reduce the drop -out rate. To fulfil the objectives of bringing all children in the educational premises another milestone is Sarva Shiksha Abhiyan (SSA) which has been launched in 2001-02. Many scholars think that MDM would fight against malnutrition and illiteracy simultaneously. Besides, it will eradicate many social evils like caste prejudice, class barriers, etc. The present paper has focused at length on the growth and acceleration of children's rights in India.

Status of Children at Early-age

Paternalism prevailed in India, since centuries. It got ingrained in the family and the societal system. Boys were preferred. A woman's status depended on the number of sons she gave birth to. In India, a child was taken care primarily, by the mother, the immediate family, or the joint family; and secondarily, by the jati (caste) or the community. (Kakar, 1982) In Ramayana and Mahabharata, instances of intense parental longing for children and society's view of childhood have been reflected. (Bhakhry, 2006) In the Laws of Manu, the child was conferred with society's protection and efforts were there towards an all-round development of the personality of the child. In ancient period, children, especially belonging to the upper castes, gained knowledge, wisdom and learnt the life skills required for a healthy and prosperous life through the *Gurukul* system. Historically, upbringing of children was affected by the biases based on socio-cultural factors, like caste, kinship, gender, etc. Emperors, like Ashoka and Chandragupta Vikramaditya had moral edicts which supported obedience towards parents and respect for elders. (Bhakhry, 2006) Classical Sanskrit literature like Kalidasa's *Abhigyan Sakuntalam* paternal love towards the male child has been elaborated. The *Bhakti* literature also focuses on the child to be at the centre of an admiring circle of adults. The medieval period saw the slow ebbing of emphasis on education of children. Elementary education got confined to the higher varnas like *Brahmins, Kshatriyas* and *Vaishyas* among the Hindus and the aristocratic and rich families at home through the *Maulvis,* among the Muslims. Muslim boys belonging to ordinary families had to go to the *maktabs* situated in mosques. Girls' education went to the back seat.

Status of Children at Early-age

History tells us that the concept of paternal authority and control prevailed in India since times immemorial. Traditionally the Indian welfare vision is based on *daya* (mercy), *dana* (charity), *dakshina* (paying tribute), *bhiksha* (alms giving), *ahimsa* (non-violence), *samya-bhava* (equality), *swadharma* (practicing religion) and *tyaga* (sacrifice). (Bajpai, 2006) The major caretaker of a child was the mother, the immediate family or, at best, the joint family; and secondarily, the jati (caste) relationships. (Kakar, 1982) An intense parental longing for children and society's view of childhood had been reflected in the Ramayana and the Mahabharata, though boys, not the girls, were preferred. Similarly, in the ancient Indian law, especially in the Laws of Manu, the child, though placed very near the bottom of a social pyramid, was conferred with society's protection. Not only protection, concerted efforts were there towards an all-round development of children's personality. Among these, education was accorded with a great significance. We frequently come across such terms as *Brahmacharya, Gurukul* etc. in ancient literature, which inform us from where children, especially belonging to the upper varnas, used to gain knowledge, develop their wisdom and learn the skills necessary to lead a healthy and prosperous life. Although historical documents point out at the persistent biases of that time in the upbringing of children from different socio-cultural dimensions like caste, kinship, age, gender, etc. rulers like Ashoka (268-31 B.C.), Chandragupta Vikramaditya (375-415 A.D.) tried to "propound moral edicts as a counter-balance in which obedience towards parents and respect for elders was extolled" (Bhakhry, 2006). Classical Sanskrit literature reflects parental love for offspring, particularly the sons. An exception, perhaps, is found in Kalidasa's *Abhigyan Sakuntalam* where sage Kanva's love for his adopted daughter, Shakuntala exceedes all the limits of paternal affection towards male child. In the *Bhakti* literature also we find the child at the centre of an admiring circle of adults. The *gopis* of Gokul and the citizens of Ayodhya – milling around little Krishna and Rama respectively, depict it. These themes expose the child's primary need to be central to his or her own world. In the medieval period emphasis on children's education which has been quite widespread earlier gradually withered away. Among the Hindus, elementary education has been mostly confined to the higher varnas like *Brahmins*, *Kshatriyas* and *Vaishyas*. But elementary education among the Muslims has confined to the aristocratic and rich families at home through the *Maulvis*. Others had to go to the *maktabs* situated in mosques. Girls, on the contrary, were rarely given education and their status in comparison to boys remained inferior.

Status of Children in the Pre-independence Period

Initially leaders and philosophers like Raja Rammohan Roy, Pandit Iswar Chandra Vidyasagar etc. took enormous initiatives to bring the then Indian society out of the prevailing social evils like, child marriage, *Satidaha* (forcible immolation of the wives in the funeral pyre of their husbands), illiteracy etc. Among the manifold attempts at social reforms undertaken by such stalwarts, spread of education, especially, for the girl child occupied an important place. Later on

Rabindranath Tagore, Swami Vivekananda and his close associate Sister Nivedita (originally Margarate E. Nobel) worked relentlessly to consolidate the spirit of Indian nationalism. Education, needless to mention, featured quite prominently in their endeavour. In the field of politics too, education, especially the need to spread elementary education was realized by Mahatma Gandhi. He stressed upon *Buniyadi Siksha* (fundamental or elementary education) and considered it as a prerequisite for the successful launching of freedom struggle (1969). To him spread of education was a necessary condition for the successful emergence of Indian nation and nationalism. Such forerunners of Indian nationalism worked obstinately for the overall development of India and the spread of elementary education acquired the centre stage in it.

Indian Education Commission

The efforts of such visionaries resulted in the formation of the Indian Education Commission by the British colonisers. The Commission, appointed in 1882, proposed a law for universal compulsory education. Its scope covered the need of spreading elementary education among children in general and for those employed in factories; in particular. The first experiment towards making primary education compulsory took place in 1893. Maharaj Sayajirao Gaekwad, the ruler of the state of Baroda, introduced compulsory education in the Amreli Division of his state. Since the results were promising, he extended it to the entire state in 1906 A.D. The first definite claim for the official introduction of primary education can be attributed to the demand by Gopal Krishna Gokhale in March 1910 of a resolution in the Imperial Legislative Council. The British Government then was not ready to accept the principle of compulsory primary education but desired to expand it on 'a voluntary basis'. The effort of Vithalbhai Patel succeeded in the passing of Primary Education Act in Bombay in 1918. This Act allowed the municipalities to introduce compulsory primary education in their areas. Other provinces also enacted laws which aimed at compulsory education within a few years. By the early 1930s, the principle of compulsory education was written into state law. Due to many reasons like technical flaws, lack of experience, unwillingness to make use of the power of prosecution under the Acts, these laws, however, could not be implemented satisfactorily.

Rights of Children Post-independence

Independence of a nation brings in new era for children, the future voters. The historical process and its socio- economic and political priorities from the mid-nineteenth to mid-twentieth century, paved the way for shaping a more consistent concept of childhood located within the family as the principal institutional influence and as the prime site for socialisation. In the same vein, the Constitution of India talks about and makes provisions for survival, development and protection of children. These are included both in "Part III and Part IV of the Constitution pertaining to 'Fundamental Rights' and 'Directive Principles of State Policy' " (Bhakhry, 2006), in which ten years commitment were adopted to ensure free and compulsory education for the children. In order to implement this and to fulfil other obligations to the children like health and nutrition, various programmes were initiated. After the enactment of the 73rd and 74th Constitutional Amendments, Panchayat and urban local self government have been made responsible for implementing different children related programmes.

After independence, the government of India followed the planned approach to national development. For this, several 'Five Year Plans' were adopted. An attempt has been undertaken to discuss these plans to find out the manner in which issues related to child development have been prioritised under its purview. One can find from the discussion to follow how, through the course of the plans, the welfare approach got gradually changed into the rights based approach towards child development.

In the First Five-Year Plan (1951-56) health, nutrition and education of children were accorded with special emphasis. The Second Five-Year Plan (1956-61) attempted to stabilize the child welfare system. The Central and different State Governments stepped in to provide the necessary safeguards to the destitute and delinquents under the Children's Act, 1960. For the training, educational upliftment and rehabilitation of the handicapped children certain special programmes were also undertaken. While the First and Second Plan focused on delinquent and challenged children, the Third Plan (1961-66) tried to integrate health and education with welfare services. Hence, the rights of all children have been taken care of. As a corollary to this the Applied Nutrition Programme was introduced in 1963. Realising the need of education at primary, middle and high school levels, the Third Plan set-up an Education Commission under the Chairmanship of Dr. D.S. Kothari, the recommendations of which led to the formulation of the National Education Policy in 1968.The comprehensive Scheme of Family and Child Welfare (1967) formed on the basis of the recommendations of the Committee on Child Care provided integrated services to pre-school children in villages and basic training to women in health education, nutrition and other related issues.

Kothari Commission

The government of India set up a number of education commissions after independence. Among these, the Radhakrishnan Commission dealt with university education and the Mudaliar Commission with secondary education. During the Third Plan, the Education Commission (1966) popularly known to be the Kothari Commission was set up under the Chairmanship of Dr. D.S. Kothari, the then Chairman of the University Grants Commission (U.G.C.). It contributed significantly to the issue of financing of education and is quite aptly regarded to be the 'turning point in India's educational life'.

Uniqueness of the Commission

Education is conceived as a pivot of national progress. Keeping this in the purview, the Commission did not confine itself to the enquiry of specific sectors of education, but attempted a comprehensive review of the Entire Education System. Greater importance was given to education in agriculture, science, industrial and technological subjects. In place of bookish education, emphasis was given to the acquisition of practical knowledge and skill. Effort was undertaken to make education job oriented because the commission realised that once the youngsters have the possibility of having job by educating themselves they would abide by the values of the society. In this direction the report of the Commission was an excellent document on education.

The programmes proposed in this report are:

(i) Internal transformation of the educational system to relate to the life, needs and aspiration of the nation,

(ii) Qualitative improvement of education so that standards achieved are adequate, keeping a continuous upward rising and

(iii) Expansion of educational facilities on the basis of man power needs and with an accent on equalization of educational opportunities.

Impact of Kothari Commission

The impact of Kothari Commission has made the provision of the forthcoming plan. The Fourth Five-Year Plan (1969-74) focused upon

> "free and compulsory education to all children up to the age of 14 years; provision of non-formal education, encouragement of physical education and other types of recreational as well as cultural and scientific activities in schools and community centres; provision of special assistance to children belonging to the weaker sections of society; upliftment of children in distress; protection

against neglect, cruelty and exploitation of children; protection against child labour; provision of special facilities for children ailing from various kinds of disabilities and encouragement and assistance to gifted children especially those belonging to the weaker sections of the society". (4th Five Year Plan, 2013)

To implement these actions, the Policy gave special acknowledgment to the role of voluntary organisations. 'Right to Health' being a basic human right was also recognised in this plan.

There has been a dramatic shift in The Fifth Five-Year Plan (1974-79) from child welfare to child development wherein importance was laid on the introduction of new schemes for children. The implementation of National Policy for Children led to the constitution of the National Children's Board in December, 1974 to meet the needs of children. The scheme of Integrated Child Development Services (ICDS), which provides preschool education for 3 to 6 years old children and covers many other important issues related to child development, was commenced on 2nd October 1975.The Scheme of Crèches/Day Care Centres for Children of Working and Ailing Mothers have been launched by the preoccupation Central Social Welfare Board (CSWB). In 1975, the Government endorsed the ILO Convention No. 123 of 1965 relating to minimum age for underground work. In the year 1979, designated as the International Year of the Child (IYC) by the United Nations General Assembly, initiative towards child welfare and child development touched a new height throughout the world. In India, a National Plan of Action was prepared for 'Reaching the Deprived Children'. All these gave a great motion to the on-going programmes related to children in India. Another important achievement during the year was setting-up of the National Children's Fund to provide the necessary impetus to voluntary organisations. As far as health is concerned, the Government of India signed the Alma- Ata Declaration of 1978 and exposed its commitment to the goal of 'Health for All by the year 2000', a call made by the World Health Organisation. In the area of nutrition, various nutrition intervention programmes were strengthened and expanded including the Prophylaxis against Iron and Vitamin A Deficiency Programmes. In 1976, the Child Marriage Restraint Act of 1929 was amended and in 1978, the Suppression of Immoral Traffic in Women and Girls Act, 1956 (SITA) was modified.

The Sixth Five-Year Plan (1980-85) echoed the approach and strategy adopted for children during the previous plan. The year 1981 was recognised as the International Year of Disabled and vigorous efforts were undertaken to implement various education, training and rehabilitation programmes for the physically handicapped children. In 1982, the Scheme of Early Childhood Education was brought in as a strategy to reduce drop -out rate and improve the rate of retention in schools. The Development of Women and Children in Rural Areas was another scheme that was introduced in the same year. Another important landmark in this direction was the formulation of the National Health Policy in the year 1983. During the same period the Government of India also recognised the International Code on the Marketing of Breast Milk Substitutes, adopted by the World Health Assembly, and formulated the Indian National Code for Protection and Promotion of Breast Feeding.

The Seventh Five-Year Plan (1985-90) focused on child development services. A separate Department of Women and Child Development was set-up for the first time in the Ministry of Human Resource Development in September 1985. Repealing the then Children's Act of 1960, to deal effectively with the problem of neglected children and children in conflict with law, the Juvenile Justice Act, 1986 was enacted. To implement the provisions of the 1986 Act, a Scheme of Prevention and Control of Social Maladjustment was initiated in 1986-87. The Government also ratified the Child Labour (Prohibition and Regulation) Act, 1986. In 1987, the National

Policy on Child Labour was formulated. In areas with high concentration of child labour, National Child Labour Projects were initiated. At the same time, initiatives were also undertaken to expand crèche services for children of working women. The scenario changed in the education sector when a new National Policy on Education (NPE) was adopted in 1986. The NPE considered "education as a dynamic, cumulative, life-long process, providing diversity of learning opportunities to all segments of society". (National Policy on Education, 1986)Its main purpose was to satisfy the objective of "Education for All" by providing Early Childhood Care and Education (ECCE), universalising elementary education involving various formal and non-formal methods, reducing the prevailing wastage and stagnation in schools. The policy document of NPE, 1986 declares, "Programmes of ECCE will be child-oriented, focused around play and the individuality of the child... The local community will be fully involved in these programmes." (National Policy on Education, 1986) To materialise these goals, certain new schemes were implemented like the District Primary Education Programme, 1986 and the Operation Black Board, 1987. Further, the Scheme of Non-formal Education was revised. Cutting across the barriers of class, caste, creed or gender the NPE tried to provide space for equal access to education to all. It also envisioned to get rid of the prevailing disparities in the educational opportunities by catering to the needs of the Scheduled Castes, Scheduled Tribes, and the handicapped and other minority groups. To address the problems of street children, the Ministry of Social Justice and Empowerment came up with the Integrated Programmed for Street Children.

Keeping touch with the rapidly changing global scenario and the resultant change in the overall attitude towards children the Eighth Five-Year Plan (1992-97) put its thrust on human development through advocacy, mobilisation and community empowerment while according high priority to the issues of survival and development of children. At the regional level, India actively promoted and supported the 1986 decision of South Asian Association for Regional Cooperation (SAARC) to take up the issue of children as a foremost concern, by declaring first a year and subsequently a decade for the girl child (1990-2000). At the international level, the Convention on the Rights of the Child (CRC) was approved by the General Assembly of the United Nations on 20th November 1989 and India became the signatory in 1992. With this a strong foundation was laid for initiating necessary legal and other developmental measures for protecting and promoting the rights of children in accordance with the CRC. During 1993-94, the National Crèche Fund (NCF) was formed to meet the growing demand for crèches. The NCF extended financial assistance for the opening of crèches besides conversion of the existing *Anganwadis*-cum-Crèches. A new programme to Eliminate Child Labour in Hazardous Employment by 2000 was announced on 15th August 1994. Prior to this, the Government of India joined the ILO spearheaded International Programme on Elimination of Child Labour. Subsequently, the National Authority for Elimination of Child Labour was constituted on 26 September 1994 to formulate policies and programmes for elimination of child labour. The "Health for All" strategy, adopted during this period promoted consistently for the health of the disadvantaged segments of society including the children. The Child Survival and Safe Motherhood (CSSM) programme was initiated during the year 1992-93 to strengthen Mother Child Health (MCH) services. During the time frame of the Eighth Five Year Plan the National AIDS Control Organisation (NACO) was set up under the Ministry of Health and Family Welfare to bolster the management capacity for prevention and control of HIV/AIDS. The Pulse Polio Immunisation Programme was also started in the year 1995.

Mid-Day Meal

Another remarkable contribution of the Eighth Five Year Plan was the introduction of the MDM to the children of primary schools. The National Programme of Nutritionals

Support to Primary Education was launched by the Ministry of Human Resource Development (Department of Education) with effect from 15th August, 1995 for the benefit of students in primary schools under Employment Assurance Scheme (EAS)/earlier Revamped Public Distribution System (RPDS). The scheme is popularly known as Mid Day Meal (MDM) Scheme. The children are given cooked food during school days in Government and Government sponsored Primary schools.

Probably it is the biggest scheme in the world to provide food to the children. The aim of this scheme is the retention of children in schools; universalize primary education by increasing attendance and at the same time to improve their health. (National Programme of Nutritional Support to Primary Education, 2006, [Mid-Day Meal Scheme], 2006) The pioneer of this scheme was the State of Tamil Nadu under the Chief Minister ship of K. Kamraj in the 1960s. But in 1925, cooked meal was served to children in the schools of Madras Corporation by the Madras Presidency. It was followed by Kolkata in 1927, some parts of Kerala in 1941 and Bombay in 1942. (Athreya, Bhavani, Anuradha, Gopinath, 2008) On November 28th, 2001a wake-up call was given by the Supreme Court in the form of an order directing all state governments to replace monthly "dry rations" of grain with daily, cooked mid-day meals within six months (Jaishankar, Dreze, 2005) to every primary schools including the Sishu Siksha Kendras (S.S.K.s). Government of West Bengal after certain initial hesitations introduced MDM in 2003.

In West Bengal, initially the scheme started in 1100 primary schools of five districts viz. Murshidabad, Birbhum, Bankura, West Midnapore and Jalpaiguri. Afterward it was extended to certain other districts. By the year 2010 almost 97 percent of the rural schools and 31 percent of the urban schools were brought under the fold of MDM programme. With the passage of time due to the thrust given by the state government, more urban schools have accepted this programme to lift the figure upto the level of 80 percent. The initial impact of the programme was impressive enough. The MDM quite significantly contributed to the higher attendance rates of the students in the schools. Drèze and Goyal (2003) also found out that most of the teachers were also of the same opinion. The teachers pointed out that earlier the children used to go home at tiffin time and many did not come back. At present, mid-day meals make it easier to retain pupils after the lunch break. There has been a continuous debate between the effectiveness of dry rations and hot cooked mid-day meal. The research team of the Pratichi Trust found that the debate primarily veered around the issues of class and identity. While the relatively well - off upper caste students preferred dry rations, the Scheduled Caste and Scheduled Tribe students belonging to the lower stratum of society preferred cooked meals. (Rana, 2004) The debate not only was confined to the nature of food served, it also went to the level of questioning the very purpose of the Mid Day Meal programme. The research team mentioned above also found that the working class students along with their parents welcomed the programme while their counterparts in the relatively rich upper class considered it as detrimental, if not harmful, to the cause of primary education itself. Such a dynamic interplay of class and caste structure can be regarded as a classic exhibition of the complex social reality of West Bengal in the contemporary period. This debate notwithstanding, the need to serve a more attractive and nutritious meal has been provided by the MDM Programme.

Decentralized approach was adopted in the education sphere for achieving the target of "Education for All by 2000 A.D." Following the revised National Policy on Education, 1992 and the Programme of Action, different steps were taken to expand the scope of early childhood care and education activities, and universalise elementary education. In the year 1994, The District Primary Education Programme (DPEP) was introduced as a centrally sponsored scheme in 42 districts of seven States, with the objective of revitalizing and strengthening the existing system. Under DPEP, the district was considered as a unit of planning.

Changing Attitudes Towards Girl Child

The world wide women's movement and the impact of feminism also affected the society's perception on gender discrimination. Special attention was paid on girls' care in a patriarchal society like India. During 1995, Beijing World Conference on Women, India was successful in convincing others to have a separate section on the girl child incorporated in the Beijing Platform for Action for the Advancement of Women. There was a cry to recognise the 'Girl Child' as an important target group, demanding attention of the Government for her development and to fight against the prevailing gender discrimination. Remarkable steps were taken for children in 1992 — two National Plans of Action– one for children, and the other exclusively for the girl child. These Plans of Action were oriented to achieve the goals pronounced in the 1990 World Summit on Survival, Protection and Development of Children. In a much similar vein, many States made their own State Plan of Action for Children/for the Girl Child. A few States also launched specific schemes to improve the plight of the girl child. For example, Haryana introduced the 'Apni Beti Apna Dhan' Scheme, Tamil Nadu initiated the 'Cradle Scheme', Rajasthan instituted the 'Raj Lakshmi Scheme' and Madhya Pradesh the 'Bhagyalakshmi' Scheme.

Right to Health

In the Ninth Five-Year Plan (1997-2002), a National Charter for Children was instituted to guarantee that no child remains illiterate, hungry or lacks of medical care. To ensure the 'survival, protection and development' of children, especially that of the girl child, the Ninth Plan provided serious attention to the problem of declining sex-ratio and the related problems of female foeticide and infanticide. These problems were dealt with a two-pronged strategy of both direct and indirect measures. The direct measures attempted at the effective implementation of the existing legislation, while the indirect measures were directed to change the overall attitude of the people in favour of the girl child. Health, nutrition and education are the three thrust areas where initiatives were taken to fulfil the rights and development of children.

In the field of 'Health', the scope of the erstwhile programme of CSSM was further widened into a comprehensive programme of Reproductive and Child Health (RCH) that paid special attention to child survival and other related measures. The Universal Immunisation Programme recorded significant achievements in arresting the problem of diphtheria, pertussis, neonatal tetanus, tuberculosis, poliomyelitis and measles. The unique drive of Pulse Polio vaccination launched during 1995-96 was continued to eliminate the problem of poliomyelitis. All these had a definite impact in reducing the Infant Mortality Rate. To achieve the goal of 'Health for All', the Government of India also took initiatives to provide safe drinking water and extend sanitation facilities to every village.

Universal Primary Education

In the sector of 'Education', in consonance with the National Policy on Education as revised in 1992 and The Programme of Action also gave special emphasis to the measures of Universal Primary Education during the Ninth Plan period. The country made impressive achievements whereby the number of schools increased four-fold from 2.31 lakh in 1950-51 to 9.88 lakh in 1999-2000, while the enrolment at the primary level shot up about six times from 19.2 million to 113.6 million. In 2001-02, the SSA was started with the aim of providing quality elementary education to all children in the 6-14 age group by 2010, further bridging all gender and social category gaps at primary stage by 2007. Continuous efforts were made to eradicate all forms of discrimination and violations against the rights of the girl child.

NGOs Intervention

Side by side the Government of India felt the necessity of the Non Government Organisations (NGO) sector in the successful planning and fruitful implementation of various development initiatives. The NGOs generally work with a mission for providing different medical and educational services to the disadvantaged. A good number of them also deal with children's rights. To facilitate the networking among the NGOs working on various child related issues, an NGO Cell was specifically formed in 1994. In 1998, the Government with the assistance of UNICEF launched a special service for children called Childline. This is a free telephone service that can be used by a child in need of care and protection or anyone on his/her behalf simply by dialling the number 1098. It is a "platform bringing together the Ministry for Women & Child Development, Government of India, UNICEF, Department of Tele communications, street and community youth, non-profit organisations, academic institutions, the corporate sector and concerned individuals." Street and community youth, non-profit organisations, academic institutions, the corporate sector and concerned individual. (Partnership Model, 2014) It not only responds to the needs of children but also plays a major role in crises intervention, long term care and it not only responds to the needs of children but also plays a major role in crises intervention long term care and rehabilitation. Up to March, 2013, Childline has responded to 27 million calls and is working in 291 cities. (Tele Helpline Model, 2014) The SOS Children's Villages of India is an example of a good NGO intervention as far as promotion of rights of the children is concerned. This organisation has brought forward a family approach to the long-term care of orphaned and abandoned children. Children in SOS Villages grow up as children in an ordinary family. This type of village is run and managed by a team of efficient child care workers. According to the latest available information "more than 6000 children and young people live in 33 SOS Children's Villages and 27 SOS Youth Facilities in the country." (SOS Children's Villages International, 2014)

Juvenile Justice

After a thorough review the Juvenile Justice Act, 1986 was repealed and replaced by the Juvenile Justice (Care and Protection of Children) Act, 2000. Furthermore, a review of major existing child-specific and child related legislations resulted in the identification of the loopholes in their implementation, viz. the Child Marriage Restraint Act, 1929, The Immoral Traffic (Prevention) Act, 1956. The need for a more child friendly juvenile justice system was the primary factor that led to the passing of the Juvenile Justice (Care and Protection of Children) Act, 2000.

Right Based Approach

Earlier the status of the children in India was solely dependent on welfare approach. This tendency was gradually shifting to the developmental approach during the dying phase of the twentieth century. The previous century witnessed various New Social Movements basically the movements focusing on "Rights". The beginning of 21st century echoes the same views. Now-a-days, 'Rights Based Approach' is gaining more importance. This was revealed in the Tenth Five-Year Plan (2002 – 2007) in which overall emphasis was on a 'Rights-Based Approach' with regard to 'survival, development and protection' of children. In this plan special drives were taken to ensure effective enforcement of legislations to prevent and eradicate the problem of female foeticide and female infanticide. In this context, in 2003, the Pre-natal Diagnostic Techniques (Regulation and Prevention of Misuse) Act, 1994 was amended. The amended Act is now called the Pre-Conception & Pre-Natal Diagnostic Techniques (Prohibition of Sex Selection) Act. Importance is also laid on compulsory registration of births and deaths, as visualised in the National Population Policy (NPP) 2000.

Constitution (Eighty-sixth Amendment) Act, 2002: Right to Education

With regard to education, the Constitution (86th Amendment) Act was enacted in December 2002. The Act notes, "The State shall provide free and compulsory education to all children of the age of six to fourteen years in such manner as the State may, by law, determine. (86th Amendment, The Constitution Act, 2002, 2014) The fact that Article 21A was added to the Constitution for recognising right to primary education implies that right to personal liberty guaranteed by Article 21 is now also the basis for a general right to education. In the same way, Article 45 of the Constitution has been replaced so as to provide for early childhood care and education for all children till they complete the age of 6 years. Article 51A was further modified by adding a clause – (k) – mentioning that it is the duty of the parents/ guardians to provide opportunities for education to their children/ward between the age of six and fourteen years. In view of the fact that education for children of 6 - 14 years age group became a Fundamental Right, the Tenth Plan adopted a new approach towards achieving the goal of Universalization of Elementary Education (UEE).

Since most of the programmes in the field of elementary education were unconnected in nature, the SSA was launched in 2001-02 for providing comprehensive elementary education to all children. The SSA is seen as a major vehicle for achieving the goals of UEE in the Tenth Plan period. SSA is anticipated to solve the present problems of low rates of enrolment and retention, besides high drop-out rates, especially amongst the girl children belonging to the Scheduled Castes, Scheduled Tribes, Other Backward Classes and Minorities. The components of SSA include construction of school building, classrooms, integrated education and appointment of Block and Cluster Resource Centres for academic support. The programme envisages bridging the social and gender gaps. Necessary motivation would be provided to states to enlarge the base of its accountability by involving NGOs, teachers, activists, women's organisations etc. in this effort. Through this programme, the Government aims to cover children who have never enrolled or those who have dropped out without completing eight years of elementary schooling. Centre of attention is now being given to strengthening the early joyful period of play and learning in the young child's life to ensure a harmonious transition from the family environment to the primary school. To ensure countrywide quality basic education, the Government of India, in the year 2004, imposed an Education Cess at the rate of 2 percent on direct and indirect Central Taxes. At the international level, it adopted the 'Dakar Framework for Action on Education for All,' framed in the Meeting in Dakar, Senegal, in April 2000. The framework makes a firm commitment to

> "...re-affirm the vision of the World Declaration on Education for All, supported by the Universal Declaration of Human Rights and the Convention on the Rights of the Child, that all children, young people and adults have the human right to benefit from an education that will meet their basic learning needs in the best and fullest sense of the term, an education that includes learning to know, to do, to live together and to be. It is an education geared to tapping each individual's talents and potential, and developing learners' personalities, so that they can improve their lives and transform their societies." (The Dakar Framework for Action: Education for All: Meeting Our Collective Commitments-Text adopted by the World Education Forum, Dakar, Senegal, April 26-28, 2014)

For strengthening the resource base, the need for education is obvious. The Government should continue to take complete responsibility of financing elementary education, given the constitutional directive and other considerations. Perhaps, due to this, in the Union Budget 1999-2000, education was made an important component of the 'national human development initiative'.

A low overall rate of literacy characterizes the Indian population. In India, the total literacy rate in 2011 is 74.04 percent which consists of 82.14 percent male and 65.46 percent female and in West Bengal it is 77.08 percent in which men contribute 82.67 percent and women 71.16 percent. However, there are wide variations across states, regions, castes, classes and sexes. Some of the current statistics as reported by the Ministry of Statistics and Programme Implementation are:

- In Gross Enrollment Ratio (GER) at primary level is high at 115%, and Net Enrollment Ratio (NER) has improved significantly from 84.5% in 2005- 06 to 98% in 2009-10. High GER at primary level, however, indicates the presence of over-age and under age children, possibly due to early and late enrollment or repetition. During this period, Net enrollment ratio (NER) at Primary level has shown improvement in most of the State / UTs of the country.
- The share of girls in the total enrollment at primary and upper primary level was 19% and 46.5% respectively in the year 2005-06; this increased to 48.5 and 48.1 at primary and upper primary levels respectively in 2009-10.
- In general, at the national level, the number of girls enrolled in all levels, i.e., primary, secondary and higher education is less than their counterparts. However, the female-male ratio in education has been steadily improving over the years. In primary education, the GPI ratio has gone up from 0.76 in 1990-91 to 1.00 in 2009 -10 showing 31.6% increase and in secondary education the increase is from 0.60 in 1990-91 to 0.88 in 2009-10 thereby showing 46.7% increase. (Children in India 2012- A Statistical Appraisal:Ministry of Statistics and Programme Implementation-Compiled, 2015).

The spread of primary education has been a spatial spread, wider coverage of children, an increase in infrastructure facilities and increased availability of costs of education may be too high for poor parents. Even in government schools with no tuition fees, there are other costs such as those of uniforms or text books. The PROBE (Public Report on Basic Education 1999) survey found that on an average the expenditure on books, fees, slates and uniforms for a child was Rs.318/- a year. This is a high level of expenditure related to income for many households. There have been numerous examples where children have been seen returning from the so-called 'free primary education' because they could not afford to wear proper uniforms or they did not appear for the examinations because they did not have money to buy the answer sheets for writing the examinations. In such cases, free schooling including books, uniforms, stationery, transportation and incentives such as free meals are required to overcome the problem of non-attendance. In addition, the concept of 'free education' stands for merely non-payment of fees and does not include expenses such as school uniforms, examination fees, transport etc. Thus 'free education' is not actually free and families have to incur costs on education in addition to losing out on the meagre wage that the child may have otherwise brought home.

Certainly, disciplinary practices are a deterrent to schooling. Some teachers, most of them being over enthusiastic and some with uncontrollable anger punish the children physically and mentally. Division Bench of the Delhi High Court commented that brutal treatment of children can never inculcate discipline in them. Obedience exacted by striking fear of punishment can make the child adopt the same tactics when he grows up for getting what he wants. (Srivastava, Seth, Kierk, 2013) In Delhi Schools, the High Court has banned corporal punishment. Other deterrents include rigid admission, examination schedules, formalities and procedures.

Lack of Initiatives

The history of compulsory elementary education

throughout the globe illustrates that legislation can play a positive role in ensuring universal education when the social conditions are congenial. In India in particular, and most of the developing nations in general, the effectiveness of legislations as a means to achieve 'education for all' has been unsatisfactory. The State here is yet to display the necessary political will and commitment to create the appropriate social and political conditions for the effective implementation of laws which deal with, "...the prohibition of child labour, extending school facilities for all, improving the quality of education etc. ... the law itself is outdated and divorced from ground realities." (Bajpai, 2006)

So to make children school bound a strategy of mobilization at the grassroots should be adopted. For effective implementation of laws supportive services needs to be invigorated. To meet these ends an overall environment is to be created and recreated where value of education gets the necessary social recognition.

National Commission for Children

As ratifying its agreement to the Convention, the government of India has made several attempts to bring the country up to the standard, such as organizing reviews of the existing laws pertaining to children, increasing publicity around children's issues by organizing conventions with key functionaries, the public, and so forth. A draft National Policy and Charter for Children (NPC 2001) has been drawn up. The Children's Code Bill 2000 provides for the constitution of a National Commission for Children for the better protection of child rights and for promoting the best interests of the child within the larger context of promoting and upholding values to strengthen the family, society, and the nation. Under the Bill, 'Child rights' means and includes the rights relating to survival, protection, participation, development as elaborated in the Convention on the Rights of the Child 1989 and the Constitution of India. The bill makes it a duty and the responsibility of the government to respect and ensure that the rights of the child are protected and guaranteed to every child within the territory of India, irrespective of race, nationality, colour, sex, religion, language, birth, political or other opinion, ethnic, economic or social status or disability or property. Finally the National Commission for Protection of Child Rights (NCPCR) was set up in March 2007 under the Commission for Protection of Child Rights Act, 2005. (The Commissions for Protection of Child Rights Act, 2005, 2006) It offers for the Constitution of a National and State Commissions for protection of Child Rights in every State and Union Territory. The functions and powers of the National and State Commissions will be to:

- examine and review the legal safeguards provided by or under any law for the protection of child rights and recommend measures for their effective implementation;
- inquire into violations of child rights and recommend initiation of proceedings where necessary;
- spread awareness about child rights among various sections of society;
- help in establishment of Children's Courts for speedy trial of offences against children or of violation of Child Rights.

The Eleventh Five Year Plan (2007-12) acknowledged the rights of children and envisioned an inclusive growth for all the children, cutting across the boundaries of caste, class, ethnicity, religion and gender. The 11th Plan promises to create a protective environment, which will ensure every child's right to survival, participation and development. The plan aims,

> ...to restructure and universalise ICDS, inter alia establish State Commissions for Protection of Child Rights (SCPCR) in every State, review and restructure the Rajiv Gandhi Crèche Scheme, combat trafficking, address the needs of adolescent girls, launch new schemes for catering

to the needs of children orphaned due to HIV/AIDS and ensure that State Governments frame rules and appoint Child Marriage Prohibition Officers, under the Prohibition of Child Marriage Act 2006. (Child Welfare, 2014)

The 11th Plan recognized that Early Childhood Care and Education (ECCE) "...is critical for school readiness/entry with increased basic vocabulary and conceptual abilities that help school retention. Besides, it will free the girl child of sibling care". (Report of the Sub-group on Early Childhood Care and Education for 12th Five Year Plan, 2012) Though the Right of Children to Free and Compulsory Education Act, 2009, specifies under Section 11 that "with a view to prepare children above the age of three years for elementary education and to provide ECCE, appropriate Government may take necessary arrangements for providing free pre-school education for such children". (Draft National Early Childhood Care and Education (ECCE) Policy, 2012) With compulsory quality education being made available to all children up to 14 years of age, it is expected that number of working children will reduce as 'children at school' are not 'children at work'. Children at homes would be linked to RTE (Right to Education) through SSA and provided age appropriate education. Besides, the street children would also get access to employment opportunities in future and keep them away from crime. Corporal punishment is prohibited and made 25 percent reservation for disadvantaged children in private school mandatory. Last, but not the least, education will make the children aware of their rights and give them confidence to fulfil them.

The vision of 12th (2012-17) Plan is that 'more inclusive growth begins with children' and instead of being 'put' on the growth agenda they are indeed the integral parts of it. This plan introduces a new "Child Rights Paradigm" that guarantees the fulfilment of children rights to 'survival, development, protection and participation as the foundation of human rights'. (Report of the Working Group on Child Rights for the 12th Five Year Plan(2012-2017), 2011)

Conclusion

Recently, Union Budget for 2017-18 has presented by Arun Jaitley, the Finance Minister. Budgetary allocations for children have granted 3.32 percent of the total funds. Noble Laureate Kailash Satyarthi and Komal Ganotra, director (policy, research and advocacy) at CRY expressed their disappointment regarding nominal raise for the children's welfare. (Satyarthi, 2017) Growth of children rights movement is not a new one, as various attempts have been made in different forms during this period to that period. After that the growth of Children rights movement has started from very beginning of 12th Five Year Plan. Throughout this period the children rights movement has taken its definite shape and in future gradually the children rights movement will occupy a definite place in our welfare society.

- This is part of the Ph D Thesis

References

Athreya, V. B., R.V. Bhavani, G. Anuradha, R. Gopinath. (2008). *Report on the State of Food Insecurity in Rural India.* Chennai: M S Swaminathan Research Foundation, World Food Programme.

Axford, N. (2008). Exploring concepts of child well-being: Implications for children's services". *Studies in Poverty Inequality and Social Exclusion Series*, 29.

Bajpai, A. (2006). *Child Rights in India: Law, Policy and Practice.* . New York: Oxford University Press.

Bhakhry, S. (2006). *Children in India and their Rights.* New Delhi: National Human Rights Commission.

Bhattacharya, A. (2014, May 8). Sarkare Darkar Nei Tai. *Ei Samay (in Bengali)*, p. 10.

Child Welfare. (2014, April 26). Retrieved June 13, 2018, from Ministry of Women and Child Developemnt: http://wcd.nic.in/childwelfare/reportwgdtd01032012.pdf

Children in India 2012- A Statistical Appraisal:Ministry of Statistics and Programme Implementation-Compiled. (2015, April 15). Retrieved June 13, 2018, from Institute of Objective Studies: http://www.iosworld.org/download/Children_in_India_2012.pdf

Covell, K. (2012). The Case for the Convention on the Rights of the Child from the Perspective of Child Psychology. In C. Butler, *Child*

Rights: the Movement, International Law, and Opposition West Lafayette (pp. 1-276). Indiana: Purdue University Press.

Draft National Early Childhood Care and Education (ECCE) Policy. (2012). New Delhi: Ministry of Women and Child Development.

Jaishankar, Y., J. Dreze. (2005). *Jaishankar Y.and Drèze J. (2005): Supreme Court Orders on the Right to Food: A tool for Action, 2005* . Retrieved November 12, 2013, from National Convention on the Right to Food and Work" : www.righttofoodindia.org/data/scordersprimer.doc.

John, M. (2003). *Children's Rights and Power*. London: Jessica Kingsley Publishers.

Kakar, S. (1982). *The Inner World – A Psycho-Analytic Study of Childhood and Society in India.* . Delhi: Oxford University Press.

Kosuri, S. (2013, July). *Right against Exploitation as Human Right: the Case of Cote D'ivory*. Retrieved October 5, 2014, from Global Research Analysis: http://theglobaljournals.com/gra/file.php?val=July_2013_1374044453_3e9ae_31.pdf

Matua, M. (2011). *Human Rights A Political and Cultural Critique*. Philadelphia: University of Pennsylvania Press.

National Policy on Education . (1986). Retrieved February 10, 2013, from MHRD: http://mhrd.gov.in/sites/upload_files/mhrd/files/NPE86-mod92.pdf

National Programme of Nutritional Support to Primary Education, 2006, [Mid-Day Meal Scheme]. (2006, September). Retrieved June 14, 2014, from National Programme of Nutritional Support to Primary Education, DEpartment of School Education and Literacy: http://www.schooleducation.kar.nic.in/pdffiles/mdmguidelines2006.pdf

Partnership Model. (2014, January 15). Retrieved June 12, 2018, from Child Line India: http://www.childlineindia.org.in/1098/b1cpartnershipmodel.htm

Rana, K. (2004, July 27-28). *The Possibilities of Mid-day Meal Programme in West Bengal, paper presented in the Seminar on West Bengal: Challenges and Choices, organized by the Centre for Social Sciences*. Retrieved June 13, 2018, from Right to Food: Rana K. (2004): "The Possibilities of Mid-day Meal Programme in West Bengal" paper presented in the Seminar on West Bengal: Challenges and Choices, organized by the Centre for Social Sciences, Calcutta, on 27 and 28 July 2004, source: www.righttofoodindia

Rao, J. (2007). *The History of Child Rights in India UNICEF*. Retrieved June 5, 2018, from UNICEF: http://www.unicef.org/india/children_3220.htm

Report of the Sub-group on Early Childhood Care and Education for 12th Five Year Plan. (2012). Retrieved June 13, 2018, from Ministry of Women and Child Development: http://poshan.nic.in/jspui/bitstream/DL/984/1/final%20Early%20Childhood%20Educxation%20in%20XIIth%20Plan%20-.pdf

Report of the Working Group on Child Rights for the 12th Five Year Plan(2012-2017). (2011). Retrieved May 2, 2018, from Ministry of Women and Child Development: http://wcd.nic.in/childwelfare/reportwgdtd01032012.pdf

Satyarthi, K. (2017, February 7). *Budget hike for kids-related schemes nominal: Kailash Satyarthi, CRY".* Retrieved June 13, 2018, from The Indian Express:, The Indian Express, February 7, 2017, available at http://indianexpress.com/article/business/budget/budget-hike-for-kids-related-schemes-nominal-kailash-satyarth

Srivastava, R.N. Rajeev Seth, Joan van Kierk. (2013). *Child Abuse and Neglect: Challenges and Opportunities,* . Philadelphia: Jaypee Brothers Medical Publishers Ltd.

Statistics of Children in India. (2017). Retrieved June 14, 2018, from Child Rights and You: https://www.cry.org/statistics-on-children

Tele Helpline Model. (2014, January 15). Retrieved June 13, 2018, from Child Line India: http://www.childlineindia.org.in/1098/b1a-telehelpline.htm

The Commissions for Protection of Child Rights Act, 2005. (2006, January 20). Retrieved June 13, 2018, from Ministry of Women and Child Development: http://www.wcd.nic.in/sites/default/files/TheGazetteofIndia.pdf

The Dakar Framework for Action: Education for All: Meeting Our Collective Commitments-Text adopted by the World Education Forum, Dakar, Senegal, April 26-28. (2014, January 20). Retrieved June 13, 2018, from World Education Forum: http://www.unesco.org/education/wef/en-conf/dakframeng.shtm

Wal, S. (2006). *Child Labour in Various Industries, Vol. 3.* New Delhi: Sarup and Sons.

(2014, January 15). Retrieved June 13, 2018, from SOS Children's Villages International: http://www.soschildrensvillages.in/ABOUT-US/Pages/default.aspx

4th Five Year Plan. (2013). Retrieved June 10, 2018, from Planning Commission: http://planningcommission.nic.in/plans/planrel/fiveyr/index4.html

86th Amendment, The Constitution Act, 2002. (2014, April 24). Retrieved June 12, 2018, from Constitution of India, 1950: http://indiacode.nic.in/coiweb/amend/amend86.htm

Chapter - VII

Human Rights Violation in West Bengal

— *Keya Bagchi*

Introduction

Man is born with human rights, irrespective of gender, nationality, place of residency, ethnicity, religion, colour, language, or/and any other categorization. Human rights reach out to all. All human beings are entitled to them and cannot be deprived from them. These rights are all interrelated, and go to develop the personality. Though all human beings are entitled to human rights, it is not that easy, to access them.

Universal human rights have been reinforced by law. They may be in the forms of treaties, customary international law, general principles and other sources of international law. Laws regarding international human rights set constraints on the Governments. States have to follow certain path or to refrain from certain acts. The aim is to promote and protect human rights and fundamental freedoms of all as displayed by Part III of the Indian Constitution.

Human rights do lay value on respect for the individual. It believes that each person is a moral and rational self. S/he deserves to be treated with dignity. They are universal. Nations or social groups have specific rights that are deemed suitable to them. But, human rights are those rights to which everyone deserves conceptually, regardless of who they are or where they live. They are believed to enjoy these rights simply because they are human, poor or otherwise.

However, many people do not know of all their human rights. They usually count only freedom of speech and belief and perhaps one or two others. These are important rights. The ambit of human rights is wide. Rights do provide freedom of choice and opportunity. They are behind in obtaining a job, choosing a career, selecting a spouse of one's choice and raise children. They include the right to travel even abroad and the right to work with respect in a workplace environment, free from harassment, abuse and threat of illegal dismissal. They even include the right to leisure.

In ages past, there were no human rights. Then the idea emerged that people should have certain freedoms. And that idea, in the wake of World War II, resulted finally in the document called the Universal Declaration of Human Rights and the thirty rights to which all people are entitled.

Human rights advocates, however, take the plea that, sixty years after its issue, the Universal Declaration of Human Rights is still more a mirage than a reality. They are honoured by violations in every part of the world. To protect human rights is to ensure that people receive some degree of decent, humane treatment. To deny the most basic human rights, on the other hand, is to deprive individuals of their fundamental moral entitlements. It is, in a sense, to treat them as if they are sub-human and bereft of respect and dignity. Examples are acts typically deemed "crimes against humanity," including genocide, torture, slavery, rape, enforced sterilization or medical experimentation, and willing denial resulting in hunger and starvation. The Amnesty International's 2009 World Report and other sources show that individuals are:

- Tortured or abused in at least 81 countries

- Face unfair trials in at least 54 countries.
- Restricted in their freedom of expression in at least 77 countries.

That apart women and children in particular suffer the most in so many ways, the press is not free in many countries to report abuse of rights, and dissenters are silenced, too often for good. While some way have been travelled in the course of the last six decades, much remains to be done to live up to the ideal of the Universal Human Rights.

Some Snaps of Human Rights Violation Around the World

Article 3 — The Right to Live Free

"Everyone has the right to life, liberty and security of person."

An estimated 6,500 people died in 2007 in armed conflict in Afghanistan—nearly 50 per cent civilian deaths took place at the hands of insurgents. Hundreds of civilians were also casualties of suicide attacks by armed groups.

In Brazil in 2007, according to official records, police shot dead at least 1,260 individuals—the high figure by any standards. All incidents were officially labelled "acts of resistance" was sham.

In Uganda, 1,500 people lose lives each week in the internally displaced camps. The World Health Organization have estimated the figure to be 500,000 who have died in these camps.

Vietnamese authorities unleashed at least 75,000 drug addicts and prostitutes into 71 overpopulated "rehab" camps, knowing well that it may lead to HIV/AIDS.

Article 13 — Freedom to Move

"1. Everyone has the right to freedom of movement and residence within the borders of each State.

"2. Everyone has the right to leave any country, including his own, and to return to his country."

In Myanmar, thousands of citizens were arrested, including 700 prisoners of conscience, and also Nobel Laureate Daw Aung San Suu Kyi. To stop her political activities, she has been put under house arrest for a long time. She has refused official offers of release and leaving the country.

In Algeria, refugees and asylum-seekers have been widely been ill treated. Twenty-eight individuals from sub-Saharan African countries with official refugee status from the United Nations High Commissioner for Refugees (UNHCR) were deported to Mali, after being tried, without legal counsel or interpreters. Their fault was to enter Algeria illegally. They were left near a desert town where a Malian armed group was on prey, without food or medicine.

In Kenya, authorities ignored international refugee law as they sealed the border to thousands of people fleeing armed conflict in Somalia. Asylum-seekers were ill-treated at the Kenyan border and sent back to Somalia, at gunpoint.

In northern Uganda, 1.6 million citizens were pushed into displacement camps. In the Acholi subregion, an armed conflict-torn area, 63 percent of the 1.1 million people displaced in 2005 continued in camps in 2007. Only 7,000 returned permanently to their places of origin.

Article 18 — Freedom of Thought

"Everyone has the right to freedom of thought, conscience and religion; this right includes freedom to change his religion or belief, and freedom, either alone or in community with others and in public or private, to manifest his religion or belief in teaching, practice, worship and observance."

In Myanmar, the military junta trampled on peaceful demonstrations led by monks, closed monasteries, confiscated and destroyed property, shot, beat and detained protesters, along with their family members.

In China, Falun Gong practitioners were tortured and badly subjected to other abuses while in detention. Christians were also persecuted for practising their religion.

In Kazakhstan, local authorities in a community near Almaty caused destruction of twelve homes, all belonging to Hare Krishna members. The pretext was that the home-land was illegally procured. The Hare Krishna community was singled out, for depriving their homes.

Parts of Some Reports on Human Rights Violations in India

2015 saw several major assaults on human rights in India — from draconian laws hitting at freedom of expression, to harassment and bullying of several communities and minority groups. The 2016/17 human rights report compiled by the Amnesty International identified 12 major human rights violations in India, such as, abuses by armed groups, caste-based discrimination and violence, negation of children's rights, communal and ethnic violence, extrajudicial killings, denial of freedom of association, freedom of expression, human right violations in Jammu and Kashmir, LGBT rights, violence against women. (These Were The 12 Major Human Rights Violations In India In 2015, Finds Amnesty Report, 2017)

India, the world's largest democracy, has a rather strong civil society, vigorous media, and an independent judiciary, but also serious human rights issues. The Government of India had introduced several schemes and programmes in 2015. Some restrictions were put on religious freedom, rights of women, children, and marginalized communities (World Report 2016, 2016).

Constraints on free speech and attacks on religious minorities, often sponsored by vigilante groups that claim to be supporters of political parties, is causing serious misgivings in India. In 2016, students were charged of sedition for giving vent to their views; civil liberties were dubbed anti-Indian; marginalised sections of society were made victims for allegedly stealing cows for beef; and nongovernmental organizations (NGOs) came under pressure due to India's restrictive foreign funding regulations. (World Report 2017, 2017).

Some Incidents of Human Rights Violations in West Bengal - Some Data on Violence Against Women

2012 NCRB report, points out that 30,942 crimes were committed against women. However, the figure has fallen slightly to 29,836 crimes in the 2013 report. Kolkata accounted for 4.49 per cent of the India's share with a population of 67.93 lakh women. West Bengal and Kolkata ranked the highest in influx of girls for trafficking from foreign countries.

West Bengal has a porous border with Bangladesh and incidents of girls getting trafficked from Bangladesh to the Indian State of West Bengal are rampant. Kolkata has the dubious distinction of the red light area, Sonagachi. (Gillepsie, Drury, 2015) Both the State and Kolkata recorded high number of cruelty cases against women by husbands or relatives. (Bhattacharya, 2015) West Bengal recorded 18,116 cases, Kolkata 1,005 cases. Cases of efforts of outraging modesty were also high with the State recording 4,913 incidents and the city 707 cases. In the past year, West Bengal recorded 1,685 cases of rape, 3,830 cases of kidnapping and abduction, 481 cases of dowry deaths and 577 incidents of insult to modesty. Kolkata recorded 75 rape cases, 145 cases of kidnapping and abduction, 15 cases of dowry deaths, 1,005 cases of cruelty by husband or by his relative and 412 incidents of insult to modesty. As many as 104 and 31 incidents of Immoral Traffic Act, 1956, were registered in the State and the city, respectively.

As per the 2013 report, the state has a population of 444.25 lakh girls. The State's rate of crime against women was 9.64 per cent of the country's share. Bengal accounted for 20 per cent of cases of cruelty by the husband and the relatives in India. Bengal has recorded high domestic violence rates. It is second in cases of suicide due to dowry and fourth in dowry murder. (West Bengal tops chart in domestic violence, 2015)

Every day, women are abused, beaten, burnt, killed and their very dignity violated in their homes. Domestic violence is widespread and covers class, caste, religion, education and socioeconomic backgrounds. The home is not the safest place for women, but of violence, as observed by Anuradha Kapoor, director of Swayam, an umbrella organization of 35 women activism group. (Barik, Kumar, Sarode, 2010) Unlike many states, women in Bengal can go to the police stations for lodging a complaint. But, it is not a complete healer. While the Protection of Women from Domestic Violence Act, 2005 mentions that cases should conclude within 60 days of the first hearing, it drags on for years in Bengal. Summons take months to be served in Bengal, in lien of two days. The conviction rate in Bengal for cruelty by husband and his family on married women is only 2.3% as compared to 15.6% of the National average. (West Bengal tops chart in domestic violence, 2015)

Over the past ten years, cases of marital violence in Bengal are on the rise by 235% against 110% national increase. Of the 3, 37, 922 incidents of crime against women in the country, Bengal accounted for 38,299 cases. (West Bengal tops chart in domestic violence, 2015)

The Protection of Women against the Domestic Violence Act, 2005 is a decade on, but, justice remains difficult for the victims in the absence of basic infrastructure, like adequate number of protection officers and service providers. While Swayam holds that there should be one protection officer per block, in effect, there are only 21 officers in the entire state. No registration of service providers for years has made the issue harder.

Uttar Pradesh, West Bengal and Maharashtra recorded the highest number of crimes against women among Indian States in 2015, as per the National Crime Records Bureau (NCRB) data released on August 30, 2016. With 35,527 cases reported in Uttar Pradesh in 2015, the state's share is 10.9% of the total number of such crimes in India, while West Bengal at 33,218 contributes 10.1% and Maharashtra at 31,126 constitutes 9.5% of the total crimes against women in the country. West Bengal ranked third in crimes against women, as released by the Crimes in India 2013 report of the National Crime Records Bureau (NCRB). It released that the undivided Andhra Pradesh and Uttar Pradesh, ranked first and second, respectively.

Domestic Violence

Domestic violence against females is a serious menace around the world. Sociologists and psychologists, of all hues, have condemned adverse impact on the mental, physical and social health of females. This has drawn the critical attention from the doctors and the para-medical personnel.

The World Health Organization (WHO) defined domestic violence as "the range of sexually, psychologically and physically coercive acts used against adult and adolescent women by current or former male intimate partners". Violence is often not only by the current husband, but includes boyfriends, former husbands and other family members, such as parents, siblings and in-laws.

Domestic violence against women is a curse prevalent in India and women usually try to hush it. Physical and mental torture is common in many Indian homes. As per an estimate, violence by their husbands is 45% in India. (Sarkar, 2010) Despite this widespread prevalence, such violence is not customarily acknowledged and has remained invisible. Women do not have places to go to, so they keep mum about it. Primary data collection while conducting research on violence against females is tough. Most females are reluctant to disclose information that they consider confidential and intimate. For eliminating domestic violence against females, it is critical to understand the context of violence and social constructs, which support its perpetuation. There is little empirical data on prevalence of domestic violence and its determinants in India, which needs urgent attention. It is important to understand this as a serious problem in a rural low socio-economic condition with poor educational and economic background of the females.

A cross-sectional observational study was undertaken by interviewing 141 adult and adolescent females residing in a Dearah village of Singur block, Hooghly district, West Bengal with the help of a pre-designed and pre-tested questionnaire. (Sarkar, 2010) Data were analyzed statistically by simple proportions and tests of significance (Chi-square test).

Out of 141 respondents, 33 (23.4%) adult and adolescent females in this village faced domestic violence in the past year. Among the demographic features, maximum incidence was observed, among 30-39 years age group, illiterate and unmarried females. For most of them, their husbands acted as the perpetrators (72.73%) and they reported slapping as the specific act of physical assault (72.73%). Majority of the respondents reported that opportunity of education (31.9%), being economically productive (31.9%) and better family income (23.4%) would help them to overcome the situation and they would be better placed to tackle it. This study points to the need for justified female empowerment and this call for multidisciplinary approach to develop confidence-building and public health measures, which would most effectively address the problem of domestic violence.

The reasons of violence are various factors such as power, employment and education level. Domestic violence thrives with illiteracy of the females. Most of the females are not aware of their rights. They tend to accept violence as something normal. This can be explained the fact that men culturally possess women. Manhood is associated with violence. Violence is widely accepted as a form of behaviour. Husbands justify this act that they have all rights to beat his wife. The girls before marriage are told to adjust to whatever happens after marriage. The Indian culture teaches obedience to women. Women consider opposing their husband as a sin. Besides that, domestic affairs are kept a secret, as a value. Change in power relationship within the family may yield to a more humane relationship.

This study indicates that justified female empowerment and enlightenment in the form of education, culture and economic productivity may contribute to this knotty social issue. Multidisciplinary approach to formulate fundamentally sound public health measures is essential. There is a need for sustained educational campaign, by the opinion leaders to bring about a change in the community's attitudes, especially of females themselves. Similarly, new textbook syllabus preaching equality of genders may prevent violence down the generations. Non government organizations must take a lead in supporting victims of domestic violence in the community with shelter, legal aid and awareness increase, with State financial aid. Economic and social empowerment of females may rebuild their lives. Panchayat members, village elders, community health workers, school teachers, existing women's organizations and mass media exposure in the villages, should be a strong force preventing and reducing domestic violence. Child marriage has to be fought out, as well.

Trafficking

Incidents of human trafficking is increasing during the period from 2011-2015.A total of 3517 cases were registered in 2011, which rose 3554 cases in 2012, to 3940 cases in 2013, to 5466 cases in 2014, and to 6877 cases in 2015 (NCRB).

West Bengal has been a hub of human trafficking in India, due to its complex socio-geographical position. It had the maximum human trafficking cases (669) amongst all states in India in 2013, followed by Tamil Nadu (549), Andhra Pradesh(531), Karnataka(412) and Maharashtra (345).

West Bengal topped the list of states with the maximum number of human trafficking cases in 2016 followed by

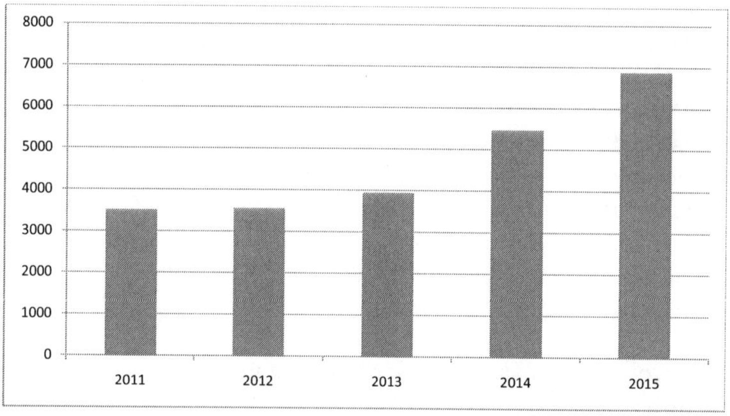

Source: National Crime Record Bureau 2011-2015.

Figure 7.1: The Number of Human Trafficking in India from 2011-2015

Rajasthan as the two accounted for around 61 per cent of such cases in the country. Of the 8,132 such cases registered across the country, 3,576 were from West Bengal and 1,422 from Rajasthan, government officials stated. ('Maximum human trafficking cases in West Bengal followed by Rajasthan', 2017)

West Bengal serves as a source, transit and destination for national and international trafficking in women and children. The state shares boundaries with north-eastern states, Orissa, Bihar, Jharkhand and Sikkim. More importantly, it shares international boundaries with the neighbouring countries of Bhutan, Nepal and Bangladesh. The geographical location of West Bengal makes it an easy prey for trafficking. Again, the social composition of state's population having the second highest density of population among the states (1028 in 2011) deserves special attention. The socially and economically backward sections like Scheduled Castes, Scheduled Tribes and Muslims forms 54 per cent of its population. Hence the State needs a multi-pronged deal to lessen trafficking. The UNICEF has already identified the districts like Murshidabad, Dinajpur (South and North), Nadia, Howrah, North 24 Parganas and Midnapur as "endemic areas of child and women trafficking". However, district wise official data on only two crime heads related to trafficking are available. They illustrate that districts like 24 Parganas (North and South), Nadia, Kolkata and Murshidabad are mostly experiencing rise in kidnapping and abduction cases of women and girls. Again, in 2005 there were 61 cases of importation of girls in the state out of which 60 were in Nadia alone and one in Howrah. Even the measures of the state of West Bengal, like, the Kanyashree are not making full inroads, in these areas.

Trafficking Routes and Prime Targets in South West Bengal

Trafficking ways and avenues are often highly complex, ranging from trafficking within one country to cross-border one. It appears from our fieldwork as well as review of literature that the border areas of West Bengal are abuzz with activity. Girls come off from Bangladesh and Nepal as well as from the selected areas within the state so as to send them across to cities like Delhi, Mumbai, Chennai, Jaipur, Haryana, Ahmedabad, or Pune. Places like Siliguri, Tufanganj, Kishanganj, Raiganj, Maynaguri, Farakka, Alipurduar, Dinhata, Balurghat, Islampur, Dalkhola, Old Malda, English Bazar, Kaliachak, Lalgola, Howrah, Sealdah, Haldia, Kolaghat, Kharagpur, Bandel, Naihati, Durgapur, Asansol, Adra, Rampurhat, Seuri, Bishnupur, and Kulti are also utilized as transit points. North Bengal has been a zone of cross border trafficking. (S.R.Mukherjee, 2005) Traffickers go on changing their base and modus operandi as per the local conditions. Hence, there may not be any fixed trafficking route. Poor vulnerable sections (poor, illiterate, landless and migrant people who lack social security) are available in different parts of the state. Majority of the trafficked girls are between 14 and 16 years, whose parents could not marry them off as they cannot pay for their dowry. 'Rupashri' is a new scheme launched in Bengal. (Das, 2018) In rural areas, the poachers live in close proximity with the recruits and also have local channels. They may be known to the victim in the form of neighbours, relatives or friends. These agents are often middle-aged women of similar social status. Sometimes, the trafficking victims themselves chip in to procure new girls from their home districts. Hence, observes Blanchet, "the traffickers exploited the trust they could easily gain from families of a similar background. They spoke the same language as their recruits. In the trafficking of girls Bengalis exploited Bengalis, females exploited females, neighbours and relatives exploited their own people." (Blanchet, 2005)

Biswajit Ghosh and Anandamohan Kar, in a study got data off an intensive study of 22 villages and other strategic locations under 12 police stations of the six districts of South West Bengal, namely Burdwan, Bankura, Birbhum, Purulia, Hooghli and West Midnapur during 2005-2006, and backed them up by similar other primary data, apart from official records and reports have identified the following trafficking routes and trafficking prone areas in the districts of South West Bengal:

(a) The industrial belt of Burdwan District, namely Durgapur and Asansol including the inter-state border areas like Kulti serve both as destination as well as out flow centre of trafficking. Girls recruited from Bihar or Uttar Pradesh, are first kept here, while girls from the surrounding districts are sent off to several hubs, as per the demand. Majority of the girls brought here from neighbouring states are lodged in the red light localities of Burdwan District.

(b) In the Eastern part of Burdwan district, girls from poor Muslim and Scheduled Caste families of Katwa and Kalna are sent across to Delhi and Uttar Pradesh via Bandel and Howrah.

(c) In West Midnapur, girls from villages in and around Kharagpur are sent to Delhi and Ahmedabad via Howrah, Ranchi or Orissa.

(d) Similarly dhabas (eatery on road side) in and around Kolaghat are developed as "safe" destinations of trafficking. There is also a trafficking link from East Midnapur to Kolkata via Haldia and South 24 Parganas. Many backward areas of both the districts serve as supply centres.

(e) There is also a trafficking route from the villages under the Taldangra and Beliatore police stations in Bankura district and the destination is Ranchi in Jharkhand via Adra. These girls are trafficked along the Grand Trunk Road. Rail links are also utilized by the traffickers.

(f) In Birbhum, the traffickers from adjacent Murshidabad district tap some of the areas under Muraroi police station to lure away girls from poor Muslim families. Khoyrasol, Dubrajpur and Seuri are three sensitive blocks that have become the hotbeds to traffickers. Birbhum is geographically close to Jharkhand and Bihar an d this provides strategic support to these gangs.

(g) Girls from certain areas of Hooghli District like Pandua are trafficked to Kolkata and Mumbai via Bandel and Howrah.

Causes and Modes of Trafficking

There are several contributing factors for trade in women and children. Even a casual look into the documents reveal that the trafficked women and girls are deployed into prostitution, pornography, petty crimes, domestic help, begging, camel jockeying, organ trade, drug trafficking etc. These poor women and children cannot get off the trade. They are physically and mentally tortured. The rapid influx of sex tourism in recent years has pushed on the demand and supply side. Women are sold at prices that vary on the basis of physical beauty and virginity. In the sex industry some clients prefer teenage girls who are perceived to be unaffected by the

AIDS. Even a girl child, sometimes as young as ten, is on high demand.

The factors of trafficking in women and children can be divided into two categories:

Push and Pull Factors

The Push factors include: poor socio-economic condition of large families, poverty with frequent natural disaster like floods, drought etc hit the people hard, lack of social and economic empowerment for women (and for their family members) in rural areas, absence of consciousness about traffickers, pressure to collect money for dowry, daughters are sent to distant places for work, dysfunctional family life, domestic violence against women, inferior status of girl child, etc,.

The Pull factors are: lucrative employment proposals in big cities, easy money, prospect and lure of better pays and comfortable life by touts and agents, demand of young girls for marriage in other regions, growing demand of young kids for adoption, rise in demand for women in the rapidly expanding sex industry etc. Urbanization provides anonymity to people coming off from the rural areas to urban employment.

Apart from these factors, weak law enforcement machinery is also a contributory factor. Some help the traffickers to recruit women and children from the districts and send them to distant destinations with relative ease. Easy bail-outs and rare conviction of traffickers encourages the operators to earn huge money without much investment. Moreover, helplessness of the victims to seek legal redress due to inadequate support from the police and the community members contribute to the spread of this crime. Trafficking along with migration, and of late, cross-border movement is on the rise. In the recent past, the demand for cheap labour, in spite of the Mahatma Gandhi National Rural Employment Guarantee Scheme, has risen everywhere in order to survive in the age of competition. At the same breath, traditional economic activities, caste occupations, age-old handicraft and cottage industries are being hit adversely by the introduction of new technology, demands for new types of consumer goods and consequent change in our cultural practices. All these factors are contributing to migration of large number of people from one place to another in search of jobs. Traffickers are aware of such events and deceive poor girls.

One major problem, faced by the poor families in India is the lack of communication outside their place of residence. Many of them are illiterate. So they depend on others for sending letters or make a phone call to their relatives. The police may not be all that supportive to these hapless girls. All this make the socially and economically backward people exposed to trafficking. It also reinforces re-trafficking often.

Globalization has played a major part for the growth of tourism business and entertainment industries the world over. As a result, sex tourism has risen rapidly. At the same time, rising male migration to urban areas, as well as stressful working of the Business Process Outsourcing (BPO) sector workers have also contributed to growing demand for commercial sex in the cities.

Trafficking is closely associated with child marriage. Child marriage is at the back of the flesh trade. It is one of the easiest ways by the traffickers to send young girls from one place to another. (National Family Health Survey, India (NFHS-II & III) 1998-99 & 2005-06, 2000, 2007) In traditional village community, there is a stigma attached to a single woman. Inability to marry off the daughter is a cause of shame for the parents. In this situation, when the traffickers approach the poor families with marriage proposal (sometimes with cash reward between Rs.1000-5000 on an average) minus dowry, the parents give in to the offer. After marriage, the girl is sold and resold, until she reaches the ultimate destination. The process has one great advantage. It protects the husband and the recruiter from the immediate accusations of trafficking. The *dalals* (agents) also shame and silence the parents efficiently by offering a share in the benefit of their daughter's sale. (Blanchet, 2005)

Apart from child marriage, there are other processes of trafficking. They are: (a) Fake marriage or marriage of a woman followed by sale to a brothel keeper; (b) Abduction or kidnapping of a girl/woman and later sold or resold to the operators of sex trade; (c) Recruitment for a job and then sold to brothel; (d) Forcing and kidnapping of children of prostitutes; (e) Luring poor families with jobs and better living condition in cities. Trafficking in women and children in recent times however happen mainly for flesh trade even though the marriage market is still there in North India and girls destined for one are often diverted to other.

Rape

Rape cases are reported almost every other day across the country, but the government figures depict otherwise. The data released by National Crime Records Bureau (NCRB) shows a 5.67 percent decline in cases of rape for 2015 as compared to 2014. The number of rape cases registered in 2015 slipped to 34,651 from 36,735 in 2014. The incidents of gang-rape have also gone down by 2,113 from 2,346 in the preceding year – a reduction of 9.93 percent. However, other sexual offences against women such as "sexual harassment", "stalking", "voyeurism", "assault on women with intent to outrage her modesty" witnessed a marginal increase of 2.5 percent. A total of 84,222 cases of these crimes were registered in 2015 as against 82, 2335 in 2014. Kidnapping of women saw a rise of 3.43 percent to 59,277 cases in 2015 from 57,311 in 2014. Forcing a woman into marriage continues to be the chief reason to kidnap her. The 2015 data discloses that close to 54% of all abductions of women were carried out to force them into marriage. In 2014 too, this reason was behind over 50% of all kidnappings of women.

As per the NCRB data, 2015, 1129 rape cases were reported in West Bengal and the state accounted for 8274 cases of the total sexual offences against women in 2015. In the category of states that reported criminal cases against women, a total of 35,527 were in Uttar Pradesh, 33,218 in West Bengal, 31,126 in Maharashtra, 28,165 in Rajasthan, 24, 135 in Madhya Pradesh, 23,258 in Assam and 15,931 in Andhra Pradesh, it said. (Over 34,600 rape cases in India, Delhi tops among union territories, 2016)

Some Cases of Rape

- A 72-year-old nun was allegedly gang-raped by around six dacoits at a school-cum-convent in West Bengal's Ranaghat at 4 am on Saturday. The nun, who was admitted to a hospital after the incident was critical and had undergone a surgery which stabilised her condition, somewhat. (Monideepa Banerjee, 2015)
- Birbhum gang rape **case** involves a gang rape taking place on January 21, 2014 in Birbhum district of West Bengal. A 20-year-old tribal girl of Subolpur village was gang-raped by a group of people, as a punishment ordered by *Salishi Sabha*, a village kangaroo court, for having affair with a boy of a different community. (Birbhum gangrape: 13 convicts get 20 years in prison for raping on order of kangaroo court, 2016)
- A minor girl was killed allegedly after being gang raped by members of a local club in West Bengal's Malda district. The body of the 10-year-old girl was recovered from an under-construction market complex, being built by the club. (Sengupta, 2017)

Child Labour

Child labour has added to the woes of the nation. Government has been taking various pro-active measures to tackle this problem. However, it is essentially a deep socio-economic problem inseparably linked to poverty and illiteracy.

To the International Labour Organization (ILO), the term, 'child labour' is often termed as work that deprives children of their childhood, their potential and dignity, and that which is harmful to their physical and mental development. It is a sheer exploitation of the young people who are often exposed to dangerous works and longer working hours preventing them from the opportunity of leading a dignified life. It refers to work that:

- Is mentally, physically, socially or morally dangerous and harmful to children; and
- Interferes with their education by depriving them of the opportunity to attend the school;
- Obliging them to leave the school prematurely; or
- Requiring them to attempt to combine school attendance with excessively long and heavy work;
- In its most extreme forms, child labour involves children being enslaved, separated from their families, exposed to serious hazards and illness and/or left to fend for themselves on the streets of large cities-often at a very early age.

According to the estimate by the Ministry of Labour and Employment (as per the Census 2001 figures there are 1.26 crore working children in the age group of 5-14 as compared to the total child population of 25.2 crore. (About Child Labour, 2015) There are approximately 12 lakhs children working in the hazardous occupations/processes which are covered under the Child Labour (Prohibition & Regulation) Act i.e. 18 occupations and 65 processes. In West Bengal there are 857087 and 234275 working children in the age group of 5-14 years in 2001 and 2011 respectively (according to 2001 census and 2011 census figures).

Child labour is found in various sectors of the society-mostly in the informal sector and unregistered one. They often work as domestic help, in small scale unorganized industries like fireworks, jewellery cutting, agricultural fields, car-washing, eateries, tea shops etc. In several states of India including West Bengal child labour is rampant in rice fields and other unorganized sectors, in spite of the legal restrictions against employing the children. The children are also put in various kinds of dangerous jobs in unprotected and unsupervised environment. This is not only illegal, but may often cause deadly diseases, which go undetected.

Poverty, illiteracy on the part of the child's family, simple greed is yet another reason of child labour. Unscrupulous employers are to hire the group of workers that is cheapest and easiest to exploit. The children are less likely than adults to know of their rights or to protest against the working conditions.

A study, launched by the Save the Children reveals sordid levels of emotional, physical and sexual abuse, domestic help in other people's homes in Calcutta. More than 50,000 children are employed in this kind of work in the Indian city and the study - carried out for four years in six districts of West Bengal - found that these children experienced abuses from unsafe working conditions, lack of food to being beaten up, deliberate burns or sexual abuse.

Save the Children hailed the Indian government's recent amendment to the Child Labour Act, but it holds that falls short in protecting children working as domestic helps. Save the Children is calling for the age limit of the Act to be raised from 14 to 18 years, as the majority of domestic workers belong to this age range. (Abuse among Child Domestic Workers: A Research Study in West Bengal, 2006)

Key findings of the research are:

- Most child domestic workers are young girls who come off poor families and are forced to work up to 15 hours a day with no breaks and little or no pay.
- 68% of the children surveyed, had faced physical abuse and 46.6% of the children had faced severe abuse that had led to injuries.

- 32.2% had their private parts touched by the abuser, 20% had been forced to have sexual intercourse.
- 50% of children do not get any leave in a year, 37% never see their families.
- 32% of families had no idea where their daughters were working, 27% admitted they knew they were getting beaten up and harassed.
- 78% of workers receive less than Rs 500 per month.

There are 10 alarming statistics on child labour, as stated by Ashwaq Masoodi:

(1) One in every 11 children in India is working. (Child Rights and You)

(2) 80% of working children are based in rural areas and three out of four of these children work in agriculture, as cultivators or in household industries, most of which are home-based employments.

(3) More than half of the 5.5 million working children in India are found in five states—Bihar, Uttar Pradesh, Rajasthan, Madhya Pradesh and Maharashtra.

(4) Adolescents doing hazardous work are 20.7% of this age group, while almost 25% of adults work in hazardous conditions.

(5) Adolescents between 15 and 17 years of age doing hazardous work, form 62.8% of the overall child labour population.

(6) Nearly 10% of adolescents working in hazardous conditions do work in family enterprises.

(7) 56% of the working adolescents are drop-outs from education. The figure is 70% for hazardous employments.

(8) More boys (38.7 million) than girls (8.8 million) are involved in hazardous work.

(9) While the incidence of hazardous work among adolescents is highest in Nicaragua, the number of

the same category is the greatest in India (2.4 million). (Masoodi, 2015)

Sexual Harassment at Workplace

In the year 1995, Bhanwari Devi, a Saathin (a village development worker) of village Bhateri near Jaipur was gang-raped by five upper caste men of the village, as a 'punishnent' for campaigning against child marriage and eventually stopping a marriage in the upper caste family. The subsequent court cases drew attention of the national and international media. Those who raped Bhanwari Devi escaped conviction. But the efforts of an NGO called **Vishaka** induced the Supreme Court to pass a historic judgement on sexual harassment at workplace. The judgement is popularly known as the "Vishaka Judgement". Vishaka had filed a petition, which sought an **enforcement of fundamental rights of working women under Article 21 of the Constitution.** At that time, law was silent against sexual harassment at workplace, so the Court issued some guidelines. It was after this case that the Supreme Court passed a landmark judgment on the issue of sexual harassment at workplace on 13 August, 1997. Recognizing sexual harassment as a human rights violation, the judgment defines sexual harassment, and puts responsibility of prevention and redress of complaints to the employer.

The U.S. Equal Opportunity Employment Commission (EEOC) defines workplace sexual harassment as unwelcome sexual advances or conduct of a sexual nature, which unreasonably interferes with the performance of a person's job, or creates an intimidating, hostile, or offensive work environment.

Between 2014 and 2015, cases of sexual harassment within office premises more than doubled–from 57 to 119–according to National Crime Records Bureau data. (Table 5.2, 2015) There has also been a 51% rise in sexual harassment cases at other work places–from 469 in 2014 to 714 in 2015.

70% working women do not report workplace sexual harassment in India. The Internal Complaint Committees are poorly trained ones. (Chachra, 2017) So, we can imagine the fate of the victims. Moreover, the Committee do not have women members. So, redressal of complaints by women, are difficult.

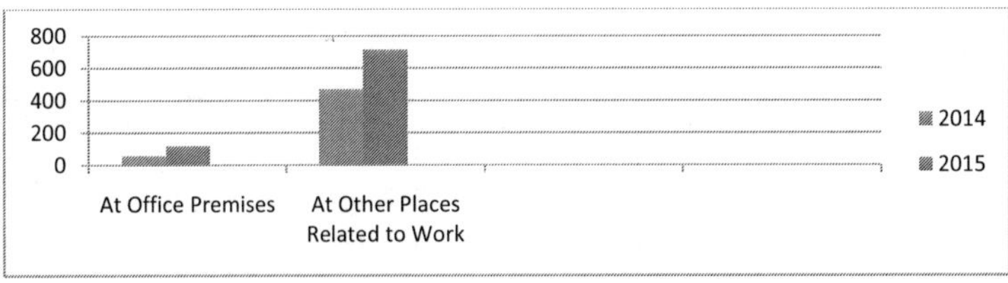

Source: Crime in India 2014 and 2015, National Crime Records Bureau.

Figure 7.2: Cases of Insult to Modesty of Women

Over the past two decades, sexual harassment is an increasing hazard globally. Sexual harassment includes overt physical behaviour, such as rape and unsolicited physical contact, as well as verbal conduct such as jokes of a derogatory nature, use of threatening or obscene language, proposals of a sexual nature, or the offer of offensive materials such as pornographic pictures, which may reasonably be perceived to create a negative psychological and emotional work environment. (Jaisingh, 2004) Sexual harassment is unwanted by or offensive to the victim to whom it is directed. In many cases, including in the workplace, the person being harassed, may not be able to withdraw from the situation easily or have recourse to help to stop or censure the offender. (Collier, 1995)

In 1997, the Supreme Court of India recognised sexual harassment in the workplace as a violation of human rights. However, little is known about the extent or persistence of sexual harassment. Some of the findings of some important studies in Kolkata and in India have been mentioned.

A survey on sexual harassment at workplace, conducted by Sanhita, in Kolkata, in early 2000, among 525 men and women belonging to the government sector (like police, railway, tax etc.), public sector (like banks, airlines, etc.) and private sector (like advertising, hotels etc.), shows that 35 per cent women had experienced sexual harassment at their workplaces. When asked about the fear of sexual harassment, 52 per cent women, while denying having faced any sexual harassment, but stated that they can face it in the future. The survey also indicates that the perpetrators of sexual harassment could be the boss/employer, colleague, subordinate, client/outsider, or just anybody from any level. When asked as to why women do not complain, most, i.e., 83 per cent, respondents indicated social stigma as the reason for not complaining, followed by fear of reprisal by 41 per cent.

To obtain an understanding of women's experiences of sexual harassment in the health sector, a study (Chowdhury, 2007) was undertaken in 2005–2006 among 135 women health workers, including doctors, nurses, health care attendants, administrative and other non-medical staff working in two government and two private hospitals in Kolkata, West Bengal, India. Four types of responses were available from 77 women who had experienced 128 incidents of sexual harassment: verbal harassment (41), psychological harassment (45), sexual gestures and exposure (15), and unwanted touch (27). None of the women complained of rape, attempted rape or forced sex, but a number of them knew of other women health workers, who had to pass through that.

Three major causes inhibited 50 of the 77 women from reporting the harassment: social norms that blame the victim, lack of awareness of their rights and, above all, recognition of power dynamics and the implications in terms of job security and risk of dismissal. Sexual norms go on to raise finger at the women for provoking harassment, on the one hand, and perceive certain forms of behaviour to be normal among men, on the other. Many young women reported that they did not complain because they perceived blame for provoking the incident or feared the loss of their reputation. Along with these social norms are unequal power dynamics. Respondents were well aware that if the offender was a person in authority, he would escape punishment, easily. Many reported fear of dismissal, loss of income, blocking of promotion and victimisation in work assignments (for example, inconvenient duty hours). Those on temporary contracts and those in the private sector especially expressed these fears. Several respondents reported that withdrawing from an unwelcome situation was preferable to, lodging a complaint. As they are not employees, their harassment may not fall within the ambit of the Vishaka guidelines.

Few respondents (20 of 135) knew of the Vishaka guidelines on sexual harassment. The hospital complaints committee for redress of complaints was not known by any. Most respondents were sceptical about the conviction effectiveness of institutionalised forms of redress, the mode of functioning of such a complaints committee, or how it might be composed.

The Indian National Bar Association conducted a survey on sexual harassment at workplace between April and October 2016. Around 6,047 participants, both male and female, and 45 victims responded to their questionnaire. Most of the respondents were from sectors like IT, media, education, legal, medical and agriculture. The respondent victims were mainly from Delhi, Mumbai, Bengaluru, Kolkata, Hyderabad, Lucknow and other areas. Around 38 percent of the respondents affirmed sexual harassment at the workplace. The survey revealed that most of the women victims took ways of their own, instead of lodging a formal complaint with the management. Fear, embarrassment, lack of faith in the redressal mechanism and ignorance were some of the reasons cited for not reporting to the management. Around 69 percent of the victims did not complain to the management fearing repercussions or retaliation. The survey also revealed that the nature of the sexual harassment involved inappropriate comments, touching and physical harassment. 65 percent of the respondents' answer was 'no' when questioned regarding following of the process by the company as prescribed under the Sexual Harassment of Women at Workplace (Prevention, Prohibition and Redressal) Act, 2013 (Sexual harassment at workplace: 69% victims did not complain to management, says survey, 2017).

Speaking at a programme on Sexual Harassment of Women at Workplace (Prevention, Prohibition and Redressal) Act, 2013" organised by Merchants' Chamber of Commerce & Industry, Chairperson of West Bengal Commission for Women, observed that the higher authorities at a workplace need to change their perception to reduce cases of sexual harassment of women at workplaces. The Sexual Harassment of Women at Workplace (Prevention, Prohibition and Redressal) Act, 2013 was passed by the Lok Sabha on September 3, 2012 to protect women from sexual harassment at work. This law is a great leap forward, as the process of remedy lies with the management. However, she also stated that implementation of the law remains an issue of grave concern. Internal Complaints Committee has not been set up in most companies, and victims had to face so much agony as well as fear for the loss of their jobs. Women get trapped in various ways in the workplace, according to the Chairperson of the West Bengal Commission for Women. (West Bengal Commission for Women: To reduce cases of sexual harassment, employers need to change thinking, 2017)

Human Rights and Globalisation

If globalization is eyed as turning the whole world into one global village, in which all people are more connected and all the fences or barriers are removed, so that the world witnesses a new state of fast and free flow of people, capital, goods and ideas, then the world would be witnessing unprecedented enjoyment of human rights everywhere because globalization is bringing affluence to all the corners of the globe, together with the spread of the highly cherished values of democracy, freedom, justice and in reality, the human rights.

On the other hand if globalization is taken as turning the world into a global market for goods and services, run by the huge multinational corporations and activated by the rule of profit, all the human rights of the people in the world, particularly in the South would be under serious threat.

Literature on globalization, in general, by both the so called advocates and opponents of globalization is abundant. However, the critics of globalization highlight erosion of human rights, particularly of the poor people and of the developing countries. Their analysis and conclusions are usually confirmed by international reports. Human rights have suffered in globalization. They usually link up the other aspect of human rights, to one or the other aspect of globalization, such as poverty in developing countries to debt or unemployment to privatization, or health deterioration to the monopoly of medicine patents. Or they enumerate the aspects of devaluations in human rights, such as poverty and lowering standards of living, increasing disparity and discrimination, denial of basic needs such as food, clean water and housing, illiteracy, etc The supporters of globalization admit that in some regions, basic human rights are not respected during the past decade. But they cite the resistance of some countries and peoples to globalization and globalization may have winners and losers. The resistance to globalization by the losers is due to their phase of stagnation and rigidity or to their traditional culture or even their religions may be anti-democratic and anti-modernization.

So both backers and critics of globalization agree on the fact that human rights are some way or the other, lose value in globalization particularly in the South. But, they differ in their analysis of facts and hence in their suggestions for remedies. While the advocates prescribe more inclusion of peoples and countries in the global system, the critics of globalization prescribe opposition and resistance of the dominance of the transnational corporations and the inequality inherent in the globalization process.

The fundamental presumption behind all UN human rights agreements were based was the State's responsibility but globalization wants the State to withdraw from public life. So a weak State cannot be a bastion for human rights.

All human rights agreements were deliberated, bargained and signed by governments and all the declarations were addressed to governments who had to be accountable for either their implementation or violations. Governments were asked to take all political, economic, social, cultural and legislative moves to translate human rights into reality. All human rights annual reports, on the state of human rights in countries of the world published by UN, human rights societies or some countries such as the USA, held government responsible for violations of human rights. Governments were assumed to be policy and decision makers for all economic, political and social sectors in their countries.

Since the Universal Declaration of Human Rights in 1948, many countries of the world, both from the North or the South, lay more stress on human rights. It is especially in the economic, social and cultural areas, policies of subsidizing food, housing and basic services such as health care, transportation, sanitation, culture and education. Many countries, particularly in the South made considerable achievements in the field of the right to employment, simply by deciding to protect local industries from competition, and thus retaining job security for their population. On the contrary, globalization pacts require governments to go by the global market mechanisms and to follow the advisories (instructions) of the international agencies such as the World Trade Organization, International Monetary Fund, and the World Bank.

So governments have to make all necessary adjustments and re-structure their societal set-ups. They have to issue new laws in every sphere to ease the free market mechanism and to cancel or amend any existing laws which go against this operation. They may even have to change or amend articles in their constitutions, such as those related to public and private sectors. Many of those revised laws relate to human rights particularly the economic, social and cultural rights. A vital section is taxation, worker-employer relations, owner-renter relations, government subsidy policy of basic needs such as food, water and housing and services such as education, health, transportation, and even mass communication and cultural services (such as telephones, newspapers, theatres, books and television). Each item is to be treated as a market commodity judged by its economic value rather than its social one.

The adoption of the wide open door policy by governments requires passing laws coming into the ways of basic human right, declared by the United Nations, i.e., the right to development. Laws allowing the free flow of capital and goods with almost no restrictions on imports through tariffs, hit hard local developmental projects.

So governments find themselves in a very queer situation. If they try to abide by UN human rights agreements which they owned up, they would be violating the globalizations pacts, which they also signed and they would be criticized or even penalized for this violation (by cutting down the aids offered to them by international institutions). If they try to abide by globalization agreements they cannot avoid violating the human rights agreements. Such dichotomy would be assailed in the human right reports and the UN statistics on human development would depict them trailing behind in indices of human development.

Governments, particularly of the developing countries, have been persuaded and coerced to leave human rights, for the sake of globalization. Violations of human rights agreements, particularly those of economic, social and cultural rights by the Companies are not punished or resisted. The reactions of both international organizations and local human rights groups do not exceed beyond criticism, condemnation or demonstrations at the most. On the contrary, violations of economic rules of globalization and agreements are harshly treated, such as economic boycotting and cutting down of aids.

Many authors provide evidence on the adverse effects of governments' adoption of globalization economic agreements on basic human rights due to the reduced overall government spending on services and satisfaction of basic human needs and the increasing tendencies towards privatization of these services.

No doubt that the widespread violation of human rights is related to the widening gap between the rich and the poor, both on the global and on the local levels. This leads to increasing feelings of deprivation and injustice among the populations of the different countries of the world which is enhanced by the rapid and unprecedented advance in communication and information technologies, which really turned the world in this respect into a global village. The deprived are exposed daily, if not every minute to images and evidences of the huge gap in standards of living between the rich and the poor.

How to Stop Human Rights Violations

There are three methods to help stop human rights violations. They are reporting violation to the Government, reporting violation to the international organization and engaging in activism.

There are another 15 ways to prevent your rights from violation (Hamzat, 2014)-

1. Know your rights
2. Never give bribe
3. Insist on your rights
4. Educate the violator
5. Be ready to commit your time

6. Never let go when you are violated
7. Expose the culprit and publish your encounter
8. Challenge your violation in court
9. Take pictures, voice or video recording to back up your claims
10. Protect the rights of others
11. Never violates others
12. Speak politely and softly, not forcefully with vulgar words
13. Be right and stay upright
14. Follow up till the end
15. Educate everyone around you.

References

About Child Labour. (2015). New Delhi: Ministry of Labour & Employment, Government of India.

Abuse among Child Domestic Workers: A Research Study in West Bengal. (2006, September 5). Retrieved May 15, 2018, from Child Rights International Network: https://www.crin.org/en/library/publications/abuse-among-child-domestic-work

Banerjee, Monideepa V. A. (2015, March 15). 72-year-old Old Nun Allegedly Gang-Raped in Bengal, State Government Orders CID Probe. West Bengal, India: NDTV.COM.

Barik, Bishnu C.Pushpesh Kumar, Usha S. Sarode. (2010). *Gender and Human Rights: Narratives on Macro-Micro Realities.* New Delhi: Rawat Publications.

Birbhum gangrape: 13 convicts get 20 years in prison for raping on order of kangaroo court. (2016, January 10). *Deccan Chronicle* . Labhpur, West Bengal, India: https://www.deccanchronicle.com/140920/nation-crime/article/birbhum-gangrape-13-convicts-get-20-years-jail-raping-order-kangaroo.

Bhattacharya, C. S. (2015, November 26). *Domestic Violence Topper for 7 years- Trafficking and Sale of Girls for Prostitution also high in Bengal: NCRB data.* Retrieved June 10, 2018, from Telegraph: https://www.telegraphindia.com/1151126/jsp/bengal/story_55088.jsp

Blanchet, T. (2005). Bangladeshi Girls Sold as Wives in North India . *Indian Journal of Gender Studies*, 305-334.

Chachra, M. (2017, March 4). *70% Working Women do not Report Workplace Sexual Harassment in India.* Retrieved May 30, 2018, from Business Standard: www.business-standard.com/article/current-affairs/70-working-women-do-not-report-workplace-sexual-harassment

Chowdhury, P. (2007). Experiences of Sexual Harassment of women Health Workers in Four Hospitals in Kolkata, India. *Journal Reproductive Health Matters: An International Journal on sexual and Reproductive Health and Rights*, 221-229.

Collier, R. (1995). *Combating Sexual Harassment in the Workplace.* Buckingham: Open University Press.

Das, M. (2018, February 1). *To study or to marry: Bengal bounty frees girls to pick and choose* . Retrieved June 10, 2018, from Economic Times: https://economictimes.indiatimes.com/news/politics-and-nation/to-study-or-to-marry-bengal-bounty-frees-girls-to-pick-and-choose/articleshow/62733946.cms

Gillepsie, Tom Flora Drury. (2015, August 7). *Inside Asia's largest red light district with hundreds of multi-storey brothels home to prostitutes - from 72-year-old women who can't bring themselves to leave, to wives fleeing violent husbands.* Retrieved June 10, 2018, from Daily Mail: http://www.dailymail.co.uk/news/article-3188393/Inside-Asia-s-largest-red-light-district-hundreds-multi-storey-brothels-home-prostitutes-72-year-old-women-t-bring-leave-wives-fleeing-violent-husbands.html

Hamzat, A. O. (2014, June 4). *15 Ways to Prevent your Rights from Violations.* Retrieved May 3, 2018, from Modern Ghana: https://www.modernghana.com/news/546444/15-ways-to-prevent-your-rights-from-violations.html

Jaisingh, I. (2004). *Laws Relating to Sexual Harassment at the Workplace.* New Delhi: Universal Law Publishing Co. Pvt Ltd.

Masoodi, A. (2015, June 12). *10 Alarming Statistics on Child Labour in India.* Retrieved May 2, 2018, from Livemint:http://www.livemint.com/Politics/ZPALzwgvOLhyMfxWsobcHM/10-alarming-statistics—on-child-labour-in-India

'Maximum human trafficking cases in West Bengal followed by Rajasthan'. (2017, March 26). Retrieved May 1, 2018, from The Indian Express: http://indianexpress.com/article/india/maximum-human-trafficking-cases-in-west-bengal-followed-by-rajasthan-4586056/

National Family Health Survey, India (NFHS-II & III) 1998-99 & 2005-06. (2000, 2007).Mumbai: International Institute For Population Sciences and ORC Marco.

Over 34,600 rape cases in India, Delhi tops among union territories. (2016, August 30). Retrieved May 1, 2018, from The Indian Express: http://indianexpress.com/article/india/india-news-india/over-34600-rape-cases-in-india-delhi-tops-among-union-territories-3004487/

Mukherjee, S.R., (2005, August 31). "Trafficking in Women and Children: Dimensions and Strategies". Kolkata, West Bengal.

Sarkar, M. (2010). A study on domestic violence against adult and adolescent females in a rural area of West Bengal. *Indian Journal of Community Medicine*, 311-315.

Sengupta, R. D. (2017, March 31). *West Bengal: Nine-year-old girl raped, murdered in Malda district.* Retrieved May 5, 2018, from India Today: https://www.inditoday.in/india/story/west-bengal-girl-raped-murder-malda-dis

Sexual harassment at workplace: 69% victims did not complain to management, says survey. (2017, January 5). Retrieved May 2, 2018, from First Post: https://www.firstpost.com/india/sexual-harassment-at-workplace-69-victims-did-not-complain-to-management-says-survey-3189524.html

Table 5.2. (2015). Retrieved May 15, 2018, from National Crime Record Bureau: ncrb.gov.in/StatPublications/CII/CII2015/FILES/Table 5.2.pdf

These Were The 12 Major Human Rights Violations In India In 2015, Finds Amnesty Report. (2017, February 22). Retrieved May 29, 2018, from Huffington Post: https://www.huffingtonpost.in/2017/02/22/these-were-the-12-major-human-rights-violations-in-india-in-2015_a_21719034/

West Bengal Commission for Women: To reduce cases of sexual harassment, employers need to change thinking. (2017, February 25). Retrieved May 2, 2018, from Indian Express: http://indianexpress.com/article/cities/kolkata/west-bengal-commission-for-women-to-reduce-cases-of-sexual-harassment-employers-need-to-change-thinking-4542546/

West Bengal tops chart in domestic violence. (2015, November 26). Retrieved May 29, 2018, from https://timesofindia.indiatimes.com/india/West-Bengal-tops-chart-in-domestic-violence/articleshow/49928756.cms

(2016). *World Report 2016.* New York: Human Rights Watch.

(2017). *World Report 2017.* New York: Human Rights Watch.

Chapter - VIII

Human Rights: Indian Cinema: A Voice to the Voiceless

— *Rwita Dutta*

Introduction

Human Rights are rights applicable to all human beings irrespective of colour, race, sex, ethnicity or any other criteria. The beginning can be traced back to World War II, with the emergence of United Nations as an intergovernmental organization, the Universal Declaration of Human Rights (UDHR) came into being. The purpose of the rights was to save the universe from further atrocities. The Declaration was drafted and laid thirty fundamental rights to ensure universal justice. The scope of the declared human rights is wide and carried in nature. The Preamble to the Human Rights Declaration demands assurance of dignity of human race, right to justice, protection against slavery, to free speech, to work, education, leisure, right to seek asylum in other countries, etc. All these are inalienable rights and considered universal in spirit. These rights have not only influenced the equalitarian states to act in accordance, but also motivated various nongovernmental organizations to subvert the society in a positive manner. The historical phenomenon like the Hague convention of 1993 further consolidated the aims and objectives of the inherent rights bestowed upon all mortal beings. Most of the nation states and its government have obligations to act as well as refrain from enactment of certain deeds considered to be anti human by the UDHR. It has been referred as mandatory for every sovereign state to protect and promote these rights.

Due to the enormous size of the population and shape of the demography, human rights in India is always in a precarious state. Though the State ensures Fundamental Rights in the Constitution of India, in practice mostly rights are violated, abused and remain unimplemented. Thousands of cases are being reported almost every other day. Free speech or freedom of expression is being violated repeatedly. State, by nature, is displaying explicit signs of fascism, especially since globalization happened to India, an increasing gulf between the haves and have nots thwarted the facilitation of basic human rights. The trickledown economics had failed to ensure economic equality, thereby producing a new set of poor class for whom white collar jobs are a distant dream for poor. The necessary prerequisite of all materialistic prosperity has been directly related to wealth. Human rights and its activism, in this situation, is in real danger. Civil society, media and other institutions have been subjugated under an array of fascist ideology and growing intolerance.

Dr. Lawrence Britt in his article "Fascism Anyone" (Britt, 2003) laid down few characteristics of a fascist state. That includes a government with jingoism, hyper nationalism and constant violation of human rights in the name of internal security issue, terrorism etc. The scope of this dubious reasons are ambiguous, uninterruptable and malicious. Britt also mentioned control of mass media to be one of the prime characters of any fascist state. Religious rhetoric is another instrument common for this state. Corporate power is protected even if it curtails the basic needs of the aboriginal people of the land. For example, in the name of Vedanta, government along with the MNC's grabbed the lands of the adivasis resulting in the violation of human rights in Chhattisgarh. In other states also, killings of the minorities violated the very basic tenets of Universal Declaration of Human Rights. Extrajudicial killings happened in Manipur, Uttar Pradesh, Odisha and Madhya Pradesh. It becomes the solemn duty of any fascist state to protect the vested interest of the corporate power and build up a nexus of power elites.

In an interview with Karan Thapar in the programme Devil's Advocate, author and activist Arundhati Ray explains how the government of India always diverts its people from the real problems, "to clear the lands, to hand over the lands to the giant corporate to actualize the hundreds of MoU's signed" (Roy, 2015) Thus on one hand the state theoretically ensures fundamental rights on the other hand the very essence of human rights are being denied. Following the United Nations Human Rights Protection Act, India also constituted its own National Human Rights Commission of India on 12th October, 1993. The concept of Human rights is dynamic and new rights are acknowledged and implemented from time to time. More than protecting the rights, it is an utmost prerequisite to restore the rights once abused. National Commission for Human Rights is expected to intervene, inquire once human rights have been neglected and further recommend remedial measures. The organization has a responsibility to spread awareness among the masses, make proper usage of mass media, civil society, citizens and nongovernmental organizations. National Human Rights Commission further delegate the power to the State Human Rights Commission. To gain importance in the International arena, especially in areas like trade partnership, India complied with the basic rules and norms laid down by the Human Rights Commission since its adoption of Paris principles. In a complicated nation like India riddled with chasms like caste, class, religion, it is more important to safeguard the basic human rights, rather than on paper. A probe into the trajectory of the human rights in India reveals strange situations. From 1970's down to the present day, the country has witnessed several atrocities on human beings. From implementing draconian laws to curbing of freedom of expression to harassment and intimidation on civil society under the pretext of terrorism and anti national activities. Freedom of speech often faced charges of sedition, defamation. There have been numerous attacks against caste minorities, from forcible rejection of sharing public as well as private space to severe discrimination and violence incurred upon the Dalits and the down trodden. The way Rohit Vemula had been coaxed to death shook our very belief of living in a caste less society. It is a question how to ensure human rights as well as Fundamental Rights ensured in the Constitution through non-discrimination on the grounds of caste, class and gender.

If the incident of Vemula can happen in a urban elite university campus, what could possibly be the fate of remote villagers. Mukul Kesavan writes in the Telegraph "Rohit Vemula died a Dalit, abandoned by the other solidarities that ought to have rescued him : the camaraderie of student hood, the fraternity of campus life, the shared subversive delight of being young in a middle aged world. His fate reflects the rejection of fraternity in our institutions, in their hostility to reservations, their barely concealed contempt's for students on a quota" (Kesavan, 2016) From the colonial period to the Brahminical system, caste hierarchy had been consolidated and celebrated. Nicholas Dirks in his celebrated book, Castes of Mind accused that caste, under British domination became a single most powerful tool to subsume all the diverse identities of India. Moreover in the 21st century, caste politics has gained momentum in order to threaten national consensus. Dirks has also stated that since 1990 caste is started "to be used as the basis of denying rather than conferring social privilege." (Dirks, 2001)

The main focal point of the article to relate the status of human rights in India, its denial and the movements surrounding it to Indian Cinema and how cinema has responded to these ills ? Let us go back to the pre-independent era, where caste is usually used as a mean to ensure division of labor in the society. Gradually it is reduced to the practice of subjugation and inhuman exploitation of the higher caste on to the lower caste. Lately lower castes asserted their existence over series of violation of human rights over their community. Cinema as a archive of a nation has always tried to act as a cohesive force to ensure national consensus. (Mazumdar, 2007) Bollywood has tried to represent India both at home and abroad, thereby it seldom provokes the ruptures, rather it tried to iron out all the fractures of Indian social system thereby emerging as a cohesive force.

Achhut Kanya (1936/135 mns/Hindi) is one of the first of its kind to exhibit the atrocities of caste and denial of human rights. Kasturi played by Devika Rani (one of the prolific film stars with western education and founder of famous Bombay Talkies) (Kohli, 2011) was a low caste village girl in love with upper Hindu boy Pratap. Society rejects their companionship and both of them married other partners. Eventually as a victim of conjugal conspiracy, Pratap and Kasturi's husband Mani were caught in a fist cuff and Kasturi gets herself killed by a running train in to stop them. Thereby her sacrifice elevates her status from an untouchable to a martyr in the eyes of the villagers. Achhut Kanya is known to be a land mark film in Indian Cinema history as it challenged the caste system in the country. Immediately after Achhut Kanya, Post independent India saw the release of another blockbuster Sujata (1959/161 minutes / Dir. Bimal Roy). Sujata (played by Nutan) is born into a Dalit family and raised by a Brahmin couple. Based on a story by Subodh Ghosh, Sujata deals with the controversial issue of untouchability. It was a part of 1960 Cannes film festival. The way the director Bimal Roy has portrayed the character Sujata and the perennial problem of Caste system of India is commendable. Much later, Shyam Benegal's Ankur (1974) and Nishant (1975) dealt with the oppression of the higher caste. Manthan (1976), Aarohan (1982) and Mandi (1983). "By the time Shyam Benegal made his first feature the debate on the relative values and significance of form and content had begun." (Kohli, 2011).

Not only the aesthetics of cinema was undergoing a huge transformation but also the left leanings of the new breed of directors started making their mark on Indian Cinema. The social ills perceived by these directors are totally different from their predecessors, who were more idealist in their thought process. Influenced by Gandhian ideals and Nehruvian socialism, the earlier directors highlighted casteism under the garb of strong romanticism. But in Ankur (The seeding, 1974) Benegal's approach amalgamated "humanism tinged with strong ideological flavor in which caste differences, the exploitation of women and the underprivileged, were all under attack" (Vasudev, 1986) It is no more the duty of the film makers to ecologies and participate in the construction of a newly independent state with occasional probe into the social evils, but rather challenge, question and subvert the social system per se. Ankur, the film "contains explicit references to the peasants movement, initially led by the CPI(M) which acquired a national dimension following the failure of the 1971-72 harvests" (Vasudev, 1986) The casteism, poverty, exploitation of women, all were sewed to gather in the film where Surya, a feudal lord (played by Anant Nag) comes to the countryside to look after his father's estate where a low caste couple, the mute Kishtaya (Sadhu Meher) and his beautiful wife Lakshmi (Shabana Azmi) take care of him and his farmhouse. Gradually he develops an illicit relationship with Lakshmi impregnates her and refuses to take the responsibility. How with the turn of events this lower caste couple suffers in his hands and how they create several moments of revolt forms most certainly creates a complex tale of oppression. The treatment in Sujata and in Achhut Kanya was sporadic but Benegal with his vision of having a caste/class less society and gender oppression almost dedicated himself in making such films, one after another, in his decade long career, with the course of time. Benegal's approach became much more straight forward, more violent and overtly political. In Nishant and Manthan, Benegal's first trilogy is based on 'ownership and power' thereby challenging the feudal infrastructure in the country. Benegal himself attributed the success of the new cinema to the existence of a demand "political cinema will only emerge when there is a need for it". (Datta, 2010) Though Ankur was set in 1945, the peasant insurrection of 1970's gave it a contemporary edge. Benegal is the first filmmaker in Hindi film industry, even if is not main stream, who consistently and coherently addressed the dalit question in his films. He used his cinema as a trope for social change. Within the democratic set up, he questions the discriminatory post colonial nation states and its policies. While Achyut Kanya was a liberal step on part of Himanshu Rai to comment on Caste system, Bimal Roy and Benegal were driven by their left leanings and an ideology proclaiming egalitarianism. The famous third cinema of the developing countries intends to question the inherent hegemonic domination within the society. Driven by the same urge, Benegal and his fellow filmmakers like Girish Kasaravalli (Ghatasaddrha) Samskara (Dir: P.Reddy/1970) used cinema to question the caste system and the violation of human rights. Restoration of human rights was always a part of their egalitarian agenda. They are never pedagogical; their activism is subtle but effective.

After Benegal, it was Govind Nihalani who carried the bastion forward based on true stories from the newspaper. Aakrosh is a poignant satire on the corruption of the judicial system and the victimization of the underprivileged by the powerful. Vijay Tendulkar, the prolific writer, about whom Ashis Nandy once wrote, Tendulkar never guarantees a good bedtime read- He never fails to make you feel that you have entered a dentists chamber with an undiagnosed abscess in the molars. The journey from resistance movement against a corrupted state machinery to the rising demands of restoration of human rights in India has not changed much in nature. Bhiku (Om Puri) a tribal low caste worker refutes the arbitrary commands of forest contractor and as a result the upper echelons of administration, police molests and kills his wife Nagi (Smita Patil). However an upper caste lawyer

Bhaskar Kulkarni (Naseeruddin Shah) fights his case which eventually resulted in counter violence to avoid further humiliation for Bhiku and his family. Thus Nihalani illustrated the inescapable marginalization and subjugation of the poor and the dispossessed in Indian society. He presents a complex portrait of the social entrenchment of traditional caste that arises, not out of human weakness, complacency or inertia but as a resigned impotence towards the incestuous union of power, wealth, and authority as well as the systematic intimidation and victimization-the silencing-of the under-privileged. Inevitably, it is this pervasive dehumanization that propels Bhiku's unconscionable act. A desperate coup de grace borne, not out of madness or displaced rage but a tragic sense of merciful liberation from the inescapable corruption of privilege. (Hood, 2000) The film which was made 25 years ago still has its intensity intact.

Following Aakrosh, there are few recent films which also commented upon the Dalit or the perpetual tragedy associated with caste system still prevalent in India. Being the avant garde films, the films of Nihalani, Ray and others failed to have a mass audience. Ray, inspired by Munsi Premchand's story directed Sadgati which talks about the grim situation faced by the lower caste in India. The way Dukhi, the Dalit worker is exploited by the upper caste Hindu is devastating yet relevant till date. All the characters are build in a way to explore the insensitivities of the upper castes and how the lower castes have internalized the age old exploitation. Over the years the caste issue has made a dent in Indian politics as well as Indian society. The era of sixties and seventies was a time for rebellion. IPTA (Indian People's Theatre Association) movement paved the path of protests through cultural activities and cinema was one of it. Besides the leftist cultural movement film societies came to the forefront to disseminate some sort of film culture in our country. These avant garde film makers were direct products of film societies not only in terms of the distinct sensibilities. They also increased their social political and cultural affiliations towards

Soviet and European culture as well as their ideology. Benegal's and Bimal Roy's films are the natural extension of their social consciousness. With globalization in India casteism and the violence related to it, gained momentum. Sustaining context of superstition, ignorance and social neurosis around it piled up more. After 70 years of India, the rise of Dalits in society (through reservation) and their consolidation as powerful voting blocs have not yet changed their status in the larger milieu. Recently few films have dealt with the caste issue more realistically. The young debutant directors are educated with a zeal to prove their worth. They are aware of the violation of human rights happening every now and then. And cinema is powerful enough to penetrate the mass psyche. As entertainment is the key issue in the film industry, caste identities never played an important role in the narrative cinema. But for the last few years, a new breed of filmmakers with a plethora of films appeared. Notable are:

(1) Chaurajga (2014) Bikas Mishra
(2) Court (2014) Chaitanya Tamhne
(3) Masaan (2015) Neeraj Ghaywan
(4) Fandry (2013) Nagraj Manjule
(5) Sairat (2016) Nagraj Manjule

Some of them have witnessed caste atrocities in real life and their films are the first hand experiences of everyday life i.e. while Sairat (2016) may seem to be an out and out love story with a domineering upper caste Hindu girl Archi (played by Rinku Rajguru) with a shy lower caste young boy Parshya. After much fiasco, they elope, get married and start living in a shanty. Gradually they start having a better life, a son is born. Archi calls her mother and informs about the baby. Her brothers come, hinting reconciliation. Finally both are killed as a part of ritualistic honour killings so randomly happening in any part of the country. A severe violation of human rights honour killings (a homicide of a member of a family by the family members with the belief that the victim has violated the laws of a community). Same issue has been dealt in "Love, Sex and Dhoka" (2010/102minutes/Hindi) by Dibakar Banerjee, another prolific film maker of the new wave cinema. But Nagraj is regional, he is Dalit and very much not Bollywood. He casts amateur artists and depicted a reality which is the biggest sleeper hit of the year, grossing over 100 crore worldwide and remade in every other languages. It was the Indian official entry to the Berlin film festival, Manjule takes pride in announcing "Sairat is my reaction to Bollywood." (Khan, 2017) By presenting it under the garb of a teenage love story, Manjule actually addresses the horror of the caste violence and challenges the absence of equality of rights in India. Honour killings are condemned as a serious human rights violation Art. 42 reads unsuitable justification for crimes, including crimes committed in the name of so called 'honor'. Then comes another landmark in the history of Indian cinema i.e. Masan (crematorium) is a story of ever changing cycle of life and death in the backdrop of the oldest city of the worldwide, Varanasi where the younger folk is trying to find a space of their own cutting across the age old constrictions of caste, class and gender. Deepak coming from the Dom lineage, is an engineering student, yet shackled in his familial ties, falls in love with an upper caste girl Shaalu. A story of hope, loss of it and redemption, for many years past, Hindi cinema witnessed a lower caste boy as the hero of the film and quickly empathises with him. Like Sairat, Maasan also received a standing ovation in one of the prolific international film festivals, Cannes and also received two prestigious awards. The Director is hopeful about the new generation who surely would break the shackles of the society to make space for love, humanity and individual identity combating the caste and gender divide.

Chaitanya Tamne in his significant debut "Court" (2014) commented upon Indian legal system and the hypocrisies of the middle class. The film is about a social Dalit activist Narayan Kambli who used folk music to spread his message is arrested, accused of inciting a sewage workers suicide.

It gradually unfolds the inhuman condition in which the gutter cleaners work. The irony lies in the fact that Kamble, in actuality, sings to communicate the hopelessness about a Dalit lives, not to incite another Dalit's suicide. In real life Sathidar who plays Kambli is a human rights activist and the editor of the radical Nagpur based publication, 'Vidrohi'. The songs he sang were voiced by Sambhaji Bhagat, the Dalit poet and activist who committed suicide protesting the 1997 killings of Dalit residents of Ramabai Colony, in Mumbai. The film also touches upon how draconian laws such as Unlawful Activities (Prevention) Act. 2008 and archaic colonial laws such as Dramatic performances Act, 1876 affects lives of people and our civil liberties.

The defence lawyer Vinay Vora (played by Vivek Gombler) is also a human rights activist. Shunning altogether the melodrama Bollywood attaches to the court room trial, this realistic portrayal of the condition of human rights and prolong abuse is long overdue. Thus by "assimilating styles, forms and issues borrowed from the minority alternative films" (Biswas, 2014) – a new kind of cinema came into being. Mainstream cinema is being made on social issues and emerging successful. Thus atrocities on human race in India are not only confined in Anand Patwardhan or Rakesh Sharma's powerful documentaries but it also involved Mainstream media to make films on human rights and influence the audience in India.

Epilogue

From 1990's, Dalit movements took a new turn. Caste politics resurfaced with the aim of bringing in social justice. The (in) famous Mandal Commission Report ensured reservations for the backward classes in 1989. It spearheaded education, employment and elected representatives in civic and legislative bodies. Cinema has increasingly included this fundamental human degradation as part of its content and participated in creating a shift in the paradigm in the cultural sphere. What cinema did is to attack the discrimination on the grounds of caste, class, religion and gender, cinema acted in a different manner. Since the blurring of the borderline happened all over the world, cinema in India refashioned it by assimilating the "style, techniques and themes of the minority alternative films" (Biswas, 2014) and presented it in a more palatable way to the audience in a fiercely competitive and market driven world. Thus with the turn of the century, Cinema in its myriad ways serving the coveted role of human rights advocate and being quite successful in doing so, by reaching to more and more audience, cutting across any kind of boundaries. Nagraj's acceptance with his film Sairat in Berlin Film Festival is a glaring example of this accomplishment. With this new breed of Directors, the stories of the violation of Human Rights found their way in to the multiplexes in India. The power of cinema is being justifiably used by these highly motivating directors to tell a tale from the point of view of the oppressed. Even Human Rights Film Festivals are mushrooming everywhere. Thus Indian cinema is slowly graduating into providing "voice" to the "voiceless" by pulling maximum audience, sensitizing them, herby popularizing the themes of human rights and building a kind of counter hegemony around it.

References

Biswas, M. (2014). For a Political Cinema to come. *Economic and Political Weekly* .

Britt, L. (2003). Fascism anyone?? *Free Enquiry* .

Datta, S. (2010). *Shyam Benegal, Roli books,2010.* New Delhi: Roli Books.

Dirks, N. B. (2001). *Castes of Mind: Colonialism and the Making of Modern India.* Princeton: Princeton University Press.

Hood, J. W. (2000). *The Essential Mystery: The Major Filmmakers' of Indian Art Cinema.* Hyderabad: Orient Longman Pvt Ltd.

Kesavan, M. (2016, January 28). Radical Brotherhood-Fraternity and the Republic.

Khan, S. (2017, August 27). *India on Film: Death and Deception-October &November 2017.* Retrieved May 19, 2018, from Funoon: http://www.funoon.co.uk/india-film/

Kohli, S. (2011, October 22). *Indian Cinema's Prima Donna.* Retrieved June 2, 2018, from Deccan Herald: https://www.deccanherald.com/content/199810/indian-cinemas-prima-donna.html

Mazumdar, R. (2007). *Bombay Cinema: An Archive of the City.* Minneapolis: University of Minnesota Press.

Roy, A. (2015, June 12). Devil's Advocate. (K. Thapar, Interviewer)

Vasudev, A. (1986). *New Indian Cinema, Macmillan India Limited.* Delhi: Macmillan India Limited.

Index

J

K

L

M